Tom

A gift in disguise

Tom

A gift in disguise

Henrietta Rose

FINDHORN
Press

Copyright © Henrietta Rose 1998

ISBN 1 899171 22 3

British Library Cataloguing-in-Publication Data. A catalogue
record for this book is available from the British Library.

Cover design by Phoenix Graphics, Winter Haven, Florida
Editing and layout by Sandra Kramer
Printed by WSOY, Finland

Published by
Findhorn Press

The Park, Findhorn   P. O. Box 13939
Forres IV36 3TY   Tallahassee
Scotland, UK   Florida 32317-3939, USA
Tel 01309 690582   Tel 850 893 2929
Fax 01309 690036   Fax 850 893 3442
            e-mail: info@findhornpress.com
            http://www.findhornpress.com

Contents

Foreword

This is a special book, and I am flattered that Henrietta has asked me to write a Foreword to it. I have been a friend of the Roses since they were married, and I have known Tom since his very early days. I am also a clinical psychologist, so that, in the course of my work, I have met and come to know many families in similar situations to the one described in this book. This experience makes it possible for me to endorse Henrietta's description of the sense of isolation, guilt and failure that is so often a central feature of the parenting of a disabled child.

However, this book is much more than a straightforward description of Tom and his family. Tom is no ordinary child, but nor are his parents ordinary parents. With rare insight, Henrietta has written about her own journey through life, and about her determination to 'reframe' her attitudes and beliefs so that she can value and cherish Tom for what he is. Yet she goes beyond this, for in her search for the meaning of Tom's life she also explores the relationships within the family, the role her husband Nick and her daughter Beatrice have played in enabling them all to see Tom through different lenses, and the part that Tom himself has played in shaping his own path through childhood and adolescence.

This is an important book because it tells a story of hope and of courage. It describes a variety of approaches to the development of self-esteem and spiritual awareness. It does so in a manner that can only be helpful to those searching for ways to reframe their own experiences. It will, undoubtedly, be a source of inspiration for thousands of families whose children, for whatever reason, do not grow up as convention dictates. It shows that we do not have to accept other people's estimates of our sons and daughters. It shows that, with a will, we can recognise the special qualities and the strengths of those who are disabled, and that we can build on those so that the disabled can grow up strong and healthy.

Tom's personality shines through this book, and his contribution to the growth and learning of his mother, father and sister is remarkable. This is an inspiring story, and I can say with confidence that it deserves to reach a very wide audience.

Dr John Coleman
Director, Trust for the Study of Adolescence

Introduction &
Acknowledgements

In writing this book, I am well aware that many, many people face the same or similar situations and that our story is not unique. It has been written because I hope that readers who are in the same position may gather something from our experience or may realise that they are not alone. I also hope that those who have no direct contact with disability will gain some understanding of those of us who do, and of how, perhaps, they can give help and support.

The book scans a period of twenty years in our lives — a period in which language in the area of disability has moved and changed. Words that felt comfortable to me at the start of the story have now begun to grate. I have, however, kept to the original words that fitted with my thinking at the time they were used, and by doing so I hope not to offend, but rather to show the progress I have made in my perceptions.

Through writing the book and through the thought-gathering and life-reviewing that has taken place, so much has been learnt by us as a family, and our closeness and love have been deepened. I want to thank Nick, Beatrice and, of course, Tom for their contributions and for actively encouraging me to keep writing.

Thanks must also go to Margaret Elphinstone, who sowed the original seed and supported my hesitant first steps, to Karin and Thierry Bogliolo for believing in the book from the start and to my sister Mary for reading the manuscript and encouraging me at the end. During the writing a large group of friends have shared their experiences with me and allowed me to quote them and I thank them also.

Part One

One

Another child

'You can have another child but it will be handicapped.' These words came as a shock to me and I didn't want to hear them. I was already upset, having just had another miscarriage. At home we had Beatrice, our delightful, bubbling three-year-old — a handful with her strong will, but just the kind of daughter I would have chosen. However, I still wanted a second child and was feeling acute disappointment at yet another failed attempt.

Nick and I married in 1968. It had been a whirlwind romance. Nick surprised me and proposed marriage two weeks after we started going out together. The engagement was only eight weeks long, but I had a strong sense that it was right for us to marry, almost a sense of inevitability. I had always been told that I would know when I met the right man and in fact, unexpectedly, that is how it felt. After the rush into marriage, we had planned to wait a while before having children. We had met at work in a probation office in London, while I was still qualifying, and I wanted some time to establish myself in a job and for us to get to know each other before starting a family. I had always thought that my mother and two older sisters had conceived on their honeymoons, so I assumed that having children would be easy. As soon as I wanted them, they would arrive. It didn't work out like that. After making the decision to start a family, it took six years and a miscarriage to produce Beatrice.

I come from a large family and, having achieved one baby, I took it for granted that we would have others, so I did nothing to stop myself getting pregnant once more. But again things were not straightforward. I was now on my fourth miscarriage. Each one happened at about twelve weeks, which gave me just enough time to realise I was pregnant, start to get excited and used to the idea, and think of a few names before I had to let go of it all again.

'You can have another child but it will be handicapped.' When I heard this, I was lying in bed in Raigmore Hospital, Inverness, but it wasn't a doctor giving me a prognosis for the future — it was a crystal clear voice in my head. Where it came from, I don't know. I was not in the habit of hearing voices but it didn't sound like the constant babble of thoughts that race around my head most of the time. Friends have suggested that it was the normal chatter of anxiety that besets all pregnant women about how their child will be, but all I can say is that I know those voices and this one felt much clearer than they do.

I took the voice seriously. It was a message to me from somewhere and I told Nick as soon as I was discharged from hospital. We thought long and hard about its meaning. I had not found mothering easy. Nobody really prepares you for the experience and I had never considered the implications of having a baby for the way we lived our lives. I had just presumed that I would grow up, get married and have children. That was my role in life. My training as a probation officer was just to fill in time before I became a mother. It had been a shock to discover how such a tiny bundle could take over one's life. It seems that the smaller they are, the more paraphernalia they need and the more psychic space they fill. If we were now being given the choice of whether to parent a disabled child, I decided to say a definite, 'No thanks,' on the assumption that such a being would need even more of our time and attention than most children. We would learn to be content with our one child. This would not be difficult, with her fair curls and cheeky ways. For the first time in nine years we used contraception and, immediately, along came Tom.

It was in hospital in Inverness that I heard the voice because we were by then living in a community in the north of Scotland. We had, however, started our lives in the south of England.

I was born in London and lived with my parents, one brother and five sisters in the same large and beautiful house from birth to marriage. A year after our wedding Nick and I bought our first home, a six-bedroom Edwardian house in south London. One summer, when we were sitting in the garden, I made the mistake of saying how contented I was and how I could imagine living there all my life. The effect of this statement on Nick was to unsettle him completely. This was not the life for him. Although he was doing well in his job, had a good home and a happy marriage, and belonged to a spiritual group that felt right for him, he experienced a separation between these different aspects of his life. Each had its own compartment and he wanted to find a way to combine them under one roof. He had read about the Findhorn Foundation in Scotland and immediately went to get the small booklet to show me. Things were never quite the same for me from that moment. I had always had a clear picture of how my life would be. A community in the north of Scotland was definitely not included in my plans. My expectations had been far more conventional.

We didn't move immediately. It took some years of heated discussion and the decision of our best friends, whom we had introduced to the community, to move there themselves, to drag me up there. I had married for life and if that was where Nick was going to be, I would go too. By this time Beatrice had been born and was six months old when we reached our new home, a one-bedroom caravan with no bathroom and a loo so small you could not sit on it and shut the door! Quite a change from the six bedrooms in London and a shock to my system. Not surprisingly, I wasn't very happy at the start of our time there.

My religious upbringing was confused to say the least. My father belonged to the Church of England and my mother to the Christian Science Church. As children, my sisters and I alternated our attendance between the two and once a month we were expected to go to the Presbyterian church with our Girl Guide pack for church parade. With my father,

I knelt to pray as a humble sinner. With my mother, I did the opposite, sitting to pray and reminding myself that I was the perfect reflection of God. As a Girl Guide, I struggled through two long and, to me, boring sermons. If I didn't want to go to church at all one Sunday, I was given numerous domestic chores to do instead, such as peeling the potatoes and laying the table for Sunday lunch!

By the time I met Nick, I didn't know what I believed and he took me down a very different path — away from religion and church services — to discover my own inner beliefs. However, despite the confusion, my childhood churchgoing had helped me understand that there are many varied and valid paths to God, suiting different personalities and cultures.

The Findhorn Foundation reflects this belief that there are many ways to God in that it is a spiritual community embracing all faiths, and those who go and live there need to believe that there is a higher purpose to life but that the route taken can vary. It was started on a caravan site by Peter and Eileen Caddy in 1962 and grew because others set up their caravans nearby and joined in. By 1975, when we moved there, it was well established, with about 125 members, and had various communal buildings including a sanctuary, which was the heart of the Foundation. Most community members went there daily to meditate together. In the early years of the community, Eileen would meditate at night and receive 'guidance' that gave directions on what work needed doing in the community and how the Foundation would develop. Peter would then organise the members to put the guidance into action. By the time we went to live there, individual members were encouraged to listen to their own inner promptings and major decisions were made by a core group of members through discussion and meditation.

As a working community, by 1975 the Foundation already had a wide variety of work departments and all members were expected to take an active role. I had been upset at Nick giving up his well paid job in London and, as he was now working for nothing, insisted that we share responsibility for Beatrice. We took it in turns to look after her. When she was with me, and it was feasible, I took her to work too. My first job was in the Publications department, helping print and collate the books the community produced. I also spent some time in Reception, on the switchboard and welcoming visitors, and later on I moved to the community shop. Nick began by working in the Maintenance department, mostly mending the caravan plumbing. He then moved to the Education department, arranging courses for members and guests, and also spent some time in Personnel, deciding who could join the community and where they would live and work. Everyone took turns in the kitchen and with the washing up. The community also had craft studios and gardens, the latter becoming famous for a while for their giant vegetables, grown through cooperating with Nature rather than controlling it.

It felt in many ways like attending a spiritual university. The main classrooms were the work departments. When Nick joined Maintenance, for example, the man in charge was a keen follower of the spiritual teachings of Gurdjieff. While they worked under the caravans or on the roofs of buildings, they carried alarm clocks in their pockets (this was before digital watches). Every hour the alarm would ring and they then had to notice whether they were 'awake' and focused on what they were doing or whether their thoughts were miles away. The purpose was to see if they were able 'to live in the now'. Between maintenance jobs, they would also do Gurdjieff exercises while Nick played the piano — quite a change from working in a probation office!

People old and young and from all different countries were attracted to the Foundation to take time to look at their lives and assess their values. They stayed for a few days as guests or a few months as community members and then returned to their homes to put their newly strengthened values into practice. We let our house in London in order to pay the fees. Our plan was to stay a year.

As far as openness to new ideas was concerned, Nick and I came from very different family backgrounds. He had grown up with a churchgoing father and had attended a high Church of England boarding school but this was balanced by a psychic, herbalist grandmother, an astrologer uncle and a generally free-thinking family. I too came from a church-going family but had been brought up to dismiss ideas such as astrology and herbalism as ridiculous. In the community I was surrounded by people who embraced such views and there was a constant flow of visitors and lecturers from around the world bombarding me, a middle-class, conventional woman, with strange new ideas.

I had not wanted to move there and the first few months were painful as I tried to settle in. Luckily, and rather to my surprise, I gave myself permission not to judge or dismiss anything for six months but to listen instead. In this way I was able to survive the experience. The end result was that I relaxed and made friends and, instead of leaving after the first year, we decided to stay on. By the time Tom was born, we had been there for over three years.

Being a mother of a young child in a community situation sounds as if it should be idyllic. Little shopping or cooking, a small space to keep clean, built-in babysitters and plenty of friends. In fact it didn't work like that for me. Beatrice was six months old when we arrived and I have already described the change in our standard of living. To give Bea a bath, I had to take her to another caravan, whatever the weather. There were very few children when we first arrived and a 'children should be seen but not heard' attitude still prevailed. Everyone was expected to work in a department, either trying to take young babies with them or leaving them in a playgroup when they were a bit older. Being in a small home with no cooking or shopping to fill the day and with just a toddler to talk to could be quite boring. Inevitably the best lectures and seminars were in the early evening, just when a mother is most occupied with bathing and feeding.

I likened the Foundation to a spiritual university and having a young baby to look after was as frustrating as it must be at any other university.

By the time Tom was born, a considerable shift had taken place in the attitude of the community towards children. Although I had found it frustrating to be a mother there with Beatrice, I loved living at the Foundation and Nick shared fully in all the parental duties. When I had come home from the hospital with Beatrice, he had attempted to dodge changing nappies by claiming he did not know how. I speedily pointed out that I was only a week ahead of him in this skill and from then on he was a great father.

There was a distinct contrast in the Foundation between the time when Beatrice was a baby and when Tom was conceived. We were not the only family to have settled in the community. Others had arrived and yet others had formed from members who had met there, so that when I was pregnant with Tom there were eleven other pregnant women and we met together weekly in a 'birthing group'. Everything in the community was organised in groups and there was a plethora of meetings — community meetings, playgroup meetings, work department meetings, discussion groups and even a Georgette Heyer group. (The qualification to join the latter was to have read every Regency romance she had written, but it was really an excuse to have dinner together!)

By forming a group, mothers found their voice in the community and it became recognised that we were doing a valid job as mothers and did not need to have other work departments. We started a mothers' work department, with the excuse for yet more meetings, but this also led on to a toddler group, then a playgroup and eventually, some years later, to a school. A number of the friends I made in the mothers' group in 1978 have remained among my closest friends to this day.

After the surprise of finding myself pregnant again regardless of having decided to be satisfied with one child, the pregnancy seemed very straightforward. The group of pregnant ladies would meet together each week and discuss a range of topics including breast-feeding and different types of birth. Most of the mothers in the group wanted a home birth, despite local medical resistance. In view of the difficulties I had experienced in giving birth to Beatrice, this was never an option for me. Despite Natural Childbirth classes and a determination not to have any drugs, labour with her had lasted two and a half days and culminated in an emergency Caesarean when the doctors realised that her heartbeat was faltering. Furthermore she had needed to be resuscitated after she was born. I therefore accepted from the start that there was no chance of a home birth for me and that my next child would be born in Inverness, about 35 miles away, and not even in the local cottage hospital in Forres.

Two days before I was due to give birth, Nick drove me to Inverness and settled me into the hospital. This was the practice with all the pregnant women from the Highlands and Islands who were either having their first baby or had experienced previous difficulties, because of the long journey involved if they suddenly needed expert medical care. This resulted in a ward full of large ladies anxious to go into labour — many, like myself, waiting for more than two weeks. I enjoyed the hospital food and the chance to lie around and read my books. I was one of the few English women present and, unlike most of the Scots, ordered porridge and black pudding from the breakfast menu. Nick's parents had come up to stay to help look after Beatrice and on most afternoons during the two weeks Nick and Bea would drive over to see me and take me out to tea. With this enforced rest and abundant food, it is not surprising that when Tom eventually arrived he was over eleven pounds in weight.

The agreement with the specialist was that I would be allowed twelve hours of labour but if nothing much was happening they would then perform another Caesarean — and that is what happened. Tom was indeed born by Caesarean section but was so big that forceps still had to be used to pull him out. As a result he had a rather swollen face and reminded me of James Callaghan who, I think, was Prime Minister at the time. In every other way he seemed perfect, with all the right arms and legs, and I dismissed my earlier worries of a handicapped baby as fanciful nonsense. My main thought was total surprise that Tom was a boy. My mother-in-law had convinced me that I was having another girl.

Two

First steps

It was wonderful to get Tom home. Home by now had grown. We had sold our house in London and spent part of the money on the luxury of a mobile home — luxury by community standards in those days because we had two bedrooms, two bathrooms, two living rooms and a kitchen. The second bathroom was soon converted back into a bedroom for Tom, and Beatrice, now aged nearly four, was able to have her own room.

Beatrice had been a model baby, sleeping twelve hours a night from birth. The hospital where she was born had suggested that this was why I had difficulty breast-feeding her and had insisted on supplementary bottles, which inevitably took the place of my own milk within a few weeks. Breast-feeding was definitely considered the best thing for a baby at a 'new age community', or at least that was the feeling among the group of pregnant women at the time, and I was as keen on it as anyone and determined not to supplement with the bottle. The result was that, despite following every useful suggestion from those of doctors to old wives' tales, I didn't have sufficient milk and Tom failed to get enough to eat. He lost two of the eleven pounds he was born with and was constantly hungry, waking us every two hours for his next feed. The clinic didn't seem to worry. He was already so much bigger than the other newborn babies that they encouraged my attempts to feed him myself until by the third month he had not regained his birth weight and I was strongly advised to change to the bottle. So a bottle it was and he instantly gained weight and slept better. I was left feeling terrible that I had starved him in order to fulfil my need to be a 'good mother'. Whether this had any long-term effects on him I will never know but he has certainly enjoyed his food ever since and went through quite a stretch of his childhood on the plump side.

Apart from the feeding and sleeping, Tom's early months were uneventful. It was great to have close friends with babies of the same age. Three boys had been born within a month and we regularly lined them up and took photos of them and imagined what fun it would be as they grew up together. It didn't quite work out that way.

Tom was a little slower at sitting up and crawling than the other two boys but still within the norm. For their fifteen-month check-ups, we all drove off merrily together to the clinic in Forres, Tom with his fluffy fair hair and chubby arms and his Osh Kosh dungarees, looking so smart. The journey back was rather more subdued. That visit was when we got the first hint that all might not be straightforward for Tom. The doctor was concerned that he was not piling up the bricks as well as he should. Doubt crept back into my mind and I thought again about the voice I had heard in the hospital.

There was nothing else visibly wrong. Beatrice had walked at eleven months and Tom not till he was eighteen months but even that, we were told, lay within the average. He played with the other children much as little toddlers do. As he started to walk around, he was noticeably clumsier than the others and would inevitably fall on them or their toys. As he was larger than they were, they began to object. I must have been worrying because I remember the delight I felt that his teeth were coming through faster than the other children's. This was his one achievement. Maybe it would have been easier to ignore his slow development if we had not been living in a community with such a close group of children. That, however, would only have postponed the pain we were to go through.

All mothers go through pain as their children grow up. You want everything to be perfect for them. I can easily think of occasions when things didn't work out for Beatrice and I remember how that hurt. The first time I experienced Tom being teased and rejected by his friends was when they all learnt to ride their tricycles but he couldn't master his. The community was a wonderfully physically safe place for them to grow up and venture out into life. The caravan site had been built on an old RAF runway so had wide tarmac areas for bicycling but Tom couldn't work out how to pedal. It isn't a skill that can be taught; it just happens one day when you learn to push alternate feet at exactly the right moment. It took Tom well over a year longer than his friends to master the art of pedalling. In the meantime the other boys seemed to delight in being able to get away from him. Not surprisingly Tom found this all very frustrating. He could see what he could not do but not how to do it. And this did not help his general behaviour.

In the seventies the Findhorn Foundation grew to over three hundred members and every week flocks of guests arrived from around the world to do courses and and take part in groups. In 1975 pressure on the accommodation at the caravan park was so intense that the Foundation bought a large hotel in nearby Forres where some members and many of the guests stayed. However there were still usually around a hundred people eating lunch in the community centre dining room at the caravan park. Food was placed on central tables and people served themselves. It was a good chance to catch friends or workmates with whom you needed to talk, so there was constant movement and a frenetic energy in the dining room. Someone like Tom, who was easily excitable, found it very difficult to sit still and get on with his meal. He would frequently leap up and race around the centre table or slide on his bottom on the shiny floor. If we managed to force him to stay seated he would shout or cry. As parents, Nick and I would feel the disapproval of the other diners. It was easy to imagine that half were wishing you would smack his bottom and make him behave, while if you did the other half would be equally disapproving! It was much easier at supper time as most families collected their evening meals from the community kitchen and ate at home. At times we gave up the struggle and had all our meals at home, but that was frustrating for us as lunch time was a good time to see our friends. Why live in a community if you were going to spend most of your time in a small mobile home?

Tom lived in the Findhorn Foundation for nearly four years. Beatrice, Nick and I were there for seven. Each year we decided to stay on for another one. We had good friends and enjoyed the life and the work in the community, while Beatrice was well settled at the local school. There was great variety in the daily activities of community life and, having come from London, we enjoyed the Scottish countryside and the proximity of the sea. There was a constant flow of speakers to the community bringing new, interesting ideas, some of which I took on board and some I rejected, but all had me thinking. I learnt a considerable amount about different spiritual paths and tried out a few. Meditations were held regularly and I attended fairly frequently although I never really felt I got anywhere with them at that time. I went because they were an important way of drawing the community together — and a break from the children.

Community members came and went but many of our friends are still living there fifteen years after we left. After seven years we found the pressure of community living too much and in the end we decided to return south because we needed to be a family with our own front door. We required more privacy. Just as Beatrice had been one of the early children to live in the community and the community had had to make changes to adapt to the needs of the growing families, so Tom was the first disabled child and at that stage the community was unable to make the necessary adjustments to help him fit in. His biggest problem was his overwhelming outgoingness. He seemed to lack the brakes and inhibitors that the rest of us use to help us fit in with society. Such brakes can eventually become a limiting and hindering factor in our relationships with others but they are still necessary. Anyone and everyone Tom met would be bombarded by questions and statements and he would expect their total attention and response. If they were able to meet this intense greeting, he would then often calm down. If, instead, the person tried to ignore or avoid him, he would remain fixed on them like a terrier attached by its teeth until they acknowledged him.

Looking back from where we are now, I find it hard to describe him specifically at different ages, except for the odd snapshot in my mind. On the whole he is a conglomeration of Tomminess and mostly I picture him as he is today. I asked a friend who last saw him when he was about three years old to describe how she remembered him. 'Wide open, big — a big boy for his age — with a big voice and a huge smile, with his mouth always open. He fully embraced everything in his path with great enthusiasm.'

The community was too intense and focused on its own course and future to handle his energy. I feel saddest when I think of his rejection by the community playgroup. It was run on Rudolf Steiner lines by a Dutch lady who felt that Tom could not keep up with the activities of the other children, in particular painting and using scissors. This meant that he was not able to stay with the group of children of his own age when he was already finding it hard to play with and relate to them. He couldn't keep up with them on a physical level such as playing on their tricycles or kicking a football, nor could he enjoy the same toys as they, like Lego, puzzles or board games. He would soon lose interest and start messing around and falling over them.

One of Tom's strengths was his swimming. He loved the water and had no fear of it but if we went with other children he invariably upset them with his splashing, either purposefully or accidentally. His slow speech at this stage didn't help as it sometimes made it difficult for the other children to understand him. One friend recently described an occasion that has stuck in her memory. Tom and I had come round for a visit. He rushed into the house thrilled to be coming to play with another child. Her son, despite being a year or two older, was terrified and immediately hid. She remembers that from then onwards she always made sure that her son would be out if we came to call so that Tom could play with his toys but not frighten him, or else she would come and visit us on her own. She knew Tom needed company of his own age and to this day feels unhappy about her solution to the problem but she could not, at the time, think of a better one.

In the community playgroup the other children formed even closer links with each other and so Tom became more isolated still. They all met up with Tom in the dining room and during the afternoons and weekends, but he was not 'one of them' and the other children were given no help in how to deal with him, which would have had to have happened if he had been included in the playgroup. Tom is a very sensitive person and must have been aware of my hurt and anger at the situation but I had no way of changing the decision. Retrospectively my anger has subsided. 'The community' was a collection of individuals including Nick and myself. None of us had experience of disability or knew how to help each other. We were all floundering together.

Luckily for both Tom and myself, there was by great coincidence a very small playgroup for disabled children in the town of Forres just four miles away. We could probably have searched most of the north of Scotland without finding another such group. This one had been started by a mother of a Down's syndrome child some years before and had been taken over by the local health authority. At first sight it did not look very prepossessing, consisting as it did of three small rooms in the basement of an old people's home, but the atmosphere was very welcoming and that was what we both needed after our rejection by the community playgroup — as well as the break from each other. There were seven children and seven adults, including a speech therapist, a physiotherapist and a teacher. Tom attended three mornings a week and was much loved by all the staff who were very supportive of us as parents. It just felt sad that this support was not available in the community, where even the parents close to me felt embarrassed about how to relate to Tom, especially as the Foundation aimed at demonstrating a new and better way of living together. I am, however, hopeful that if Tom had been born into the community in the nineties it would have been different, as the whole attitude to children has continued to move forward and, although I know of no other disabled youngsters there, the community is having to look at various vulnerable groups, such as the elderly, and plan how best to meet their needs.

Three

Lessons

By the time we left Scotland, Tom was nearly four years old. He still had blond hair, a pink complexion and a bit too much weight, which seemed to make him awkward and heavy in his body. His speech had initially been slow and then he developed his own way of speaking. 'Wappen if?' translated into 'what would happen if?' It seemed as if his mind was working far faster than his tongue could cope with. He was still uncoordinated and very active and was quite a handful to manage but he was developing a keen interest in the world and a great love of music. He could not be described as hyperactive because when we put music on he would lie for an hour on the sofa, clutching the cover of the record and listening intently. The playgroup in Forres was classed as an assessment centre and by the time we set off south they had filled us with hope by recommending that we place Tom in a mainstream school as soon as he was old enough. It seemed as if he was just taking time to grow into his body and was finding that understandably frustrating.

We had decided not to return to London. My parents had moved to the west country when they retired and my father had died while we were living in Scotland. Initially we moved in with my mother while we house-hunted. I was anxious about bringing Tom to live with his granny. She loves little babies and older children but had always maintained that toddlers should be put in cold storage until they reached a more civilised stage. I thought I had kept to this rather well by having both children in the north of Scotland for their first few years! The only trouble was that Tom's toddler stage was still continuing. Luckily, stupid worries like the mess Tom made on the floor when he ate, exacerbated in the Foundation dining room by the attitude of some of the community members, were unnecessary as she had two dogs who were merely instructed to hoover after every meal. In fact we had a happy time with my mother. Within three months we had moved into a house in the nearest town. We hadn't planned to live so close to her but it turned out to be an inspired choice because we became close friends and she has remained our greatest help and supporter, despite the fact that Tom has made her face lessons that have not been easy. He certainly didn't fit what I thought would be her image of the perfect grandchild.

It was March when we arrived down south. Beatrice settled immediately into a local private primary school. Tom was given a place to begin at their kindergarten in September. We then looked for a playgroup for the intervening months. The closest one could only offer him a morning a week. I worried in case this decision was made because they found him too difficult to manage for any longer, but I never had the courage to ask. At the end of the morning I would nip in to collect him as quickly as possible, so that nobody had time to comment on his behaviour.

Then came the day for him to start at the kindergarten. We had spent a vast sum on his uniform, which included a black and red tie and cap. He looked the perfect schoolboy and as we walked round the corner to the gate on the first day I was delighted. The dream of how my son should turn out was at last being fulfilled. I could see him in my mind following his grandfather, uncles and cousins to their school at Winchester. I was desperate for him to fit in.

Again, I resisted hovering around the classroom and would whisk him quickly away but after a few days the teacher asked to see us and commented that he was having difficulty in sitting cross-legged. Doubt crept into my dream again. Every day when I went to collect him I dreaded another summons from the teacher. He lasted over a term but eventually the call came from the headmaster. They were very sorry but they did not feel this was the school for Tom and, with our agreement, they would like to have him tested by the educational psychologist. We had to agree and the tests were done.

Nick and I went for the results. Nick has taken his full share in each stage of Tom's life. I show my emotions more easily so have probably expressed our joint feelings more visibly. I find it very hard not to cry when talking about anything that matters to me. It has been a thorough nuisance in my life, although I have learnt to live with it. I certainly cried through much of the interview with the educational psychologist. The upshot was that he advised us to move Tom to St Vincent's School, the local authority assessment centre for children with special needs, and said he would arrange family counselling for us. The implication was that it was not necessarily Tom who had the problems but we as parents. Aunts had previously suggested that all Tom needed was a good smack. I had to keep reassuring myself that Beatrice was doing fine and that if I could bring up one happy and healthy child then I was not a failure as a mother. Parenting is not an easy task and there is no course you can go on to prepare yourselves. I am sure most mothers have the same doubts as I had about their abilities and will understand how undermined we felt.

Tom attended St Vincent's for two years, but we were never given the family counselling. It was always put off due to lack of staff at the Child Guidance department. Although I resented the implication that the problems were ours, not Tom's, I was also looking for some support and help in how to manage him. I quite often found myself thinking that it would have been easier in some ways to have given birth to a child with more apparent disabilities such as Down's syndrome, blindness or a missing limb. It would all have been clear cut both for us and Tom. Hopefully we would have received straightforward sympathy and help. It was not immediately obvious when you met Tom that he had a problem and when we were out amongst the general public, strangers often reacted to his pushes or comments before they realised the situation. It was easier to stay at home.

Community living had not worked out with Tom. The next few years introduced us to the loneliness of living in our society with a disabled child, especially one whose behaviour left a lot to be desired. I grew up in a family where small children were kept in the nursery with their nanny and only when they reached a civilised age and behaviour were they allowed to join in with adult meals. Nor did we go on family treats until we had learnt to behave. It has left me with fairly rigid expectations about the behaviour of children despite the fact that I myself was seen as a naughty child. Times have changed and few families have nannies unless both parents are working, but the general attitude to children in the United Kingdom is taking time to alter, and bears no comparison to the open affection shown to most children in the Mediterranean countries. Nearly all mothers know the occasional agony of their child misbehaving in public. Friends invite you to meals but expect your children to be angelic. Who wants to give away precious time by inviting a family whose children argue, hit or swear, which all children do from time to time. A naughty child would have been isolating enough but naughtiness is usually a short-term problem. Tom's problems, like those of many other disabled children, did not go away. As he got more frustrated by life, his behaviour problems increased. It would have been so much easier if his problem had been given a name.

During the two years at St Vincent's many names for his difficulties were suggested and later discarded. The clumsy child syndrome, hyperactivity, food-allergy, severe dyslexia. His IQ appeared to be fine as judged by his speech, although he was pretty impossible to test at that age as he could not concentrate or sit still long enough to complete the tasks.

As a baby he had suffered a serious reaction to cow's milk, and his face and bottom had been covered with weeping sores. It went when we put him on goat's milk instead and after about five years he grew out of it. This led us to hope that his problems might be caused by food allergies. It was a time when many mothers were worrying about artificial colourings and E numbers. The GP was quite sympathetic and referred him to the hospital where the dietitian started him on the caveman diet. Poor Tom! This meant nothing but brown rice and potatoes for the first week with a form for me to fill in to monitor his behaviour. Then each subsequent week he was allowed one new item, such as bananas or cabbage or lamb. I discovered a lot about food that I didn't know previously. For example, I was shocked to discover that lamb was the only meat allowed for a long time as all the others could easily have antibiotics or artificial colourings in them. Every day I had to note down his behaviour. It took weeks and was totally inconclusive, partly because the comments on his behaviour were so subjective and partly because Tom was well aware of what was happening and if he wanted to eat something he made a real effort to behave. In fact, although it was not meant to be, it was much more of a behaviour modification programme with food as a reward for good behaviour. In the end the local hospital gave up and allowed us to take him to another hospital a hundred miles away who did skin tests for allergies. There we were told he was allergic to house dust mites, which we didn't want to know, and probably artificial colouring. That just complicated our lives because both are hard to escape from. Beatrice with her asthma struggles with the house dust mite but Tom, apart from croup as a baby, had shown no similar symptoms, so they had given us a cause for a problem he did not appear to have!.

While Tom was on these diets, Beatrice became a vegetarian and, as we were supplementing our income with foreign students in the house, most days I had three different menus to serve at the table. Despite this and the inconclusiveness of the food allergy path, we were determined to find out what was the matter with Tom and so continued a slow and laborious trail from one expert or therapist to another.

We were still hoping that if we discovered the cause, we could find a cure. We didn't question why he had a problem.

I'm not sure whether I believe in reincarnation but I do believe that we each have a soul, that before birth we choose the body and setting in which we will live and that the purpose of our life is to work at improving and hopefully one day perfecting ourselves so that we can live with God (whatever that means!). I cannot imagine that this perfecting is likely to be completed in one lifetime, so our souls may choose another body and return to this earth, or perhaps we continue in another dimension or universe. I like to keep my options open and don't feel that I can or need to know the details of the future — but I do think that every experience we put ourselves through is an opportunity to learn and improve.

I believe that Tom, before he was born, chose his body and us as his family and it is up to us to help and support him to achieve what he has come here to learn, whilst simultaneously gaining from him the lessons he offers us. One major and painful lesson for me was to allow my son to be who he is and not to try to force him into a mould that is totally the wrong shape for him. In the early years of his life, once we had recognised that he had problems, my motive in chasing a diagnosis of his troubles was the desperate hope that they would be curable, as much for my sake as for his. I so wanted my expectations of a son to be fulfilled.

Four

On our toes

By the age of seven Tom was a lively, demanding, talkative, chubby lad and he could be very endearing, although often we were too tired to see his more positive attributes. Part of our exhaustion came from the fact that he continued for years to wake frequently at night and come running into our bedroom. We partly solved the problem of lack of sleep that this created for us by alternating night duty. Each night we swapped sides of the bed so that the person nearest the door woke up to greet him and return him to his own bed, probably having to change the sheet at the same time! Before we worked out this solution, Tom would wake and we would each lie with our eyes tight shut, pretending that we were asleep and hoping that the other would get up. The one who got up felt resentful, while the one in bed felt guilty, and we were both wide awake. Once we had instituted the 'night duty system' the two of us fared much better. The sleeper got a reasonable night while the other knew it would be their turn to sleep the next night.

Tom's coming through at night was a reflection of his desire to get on with living and his wish to join in at all times. He has great enthusiasm for the things that interest him and likes to take part in everything that is going on. A friend was telling me recently of how he remembered him at dinner parties at that time. Tom would bustle into the room and run round the table dribbling and tremendously animated. His constant talking left no time for swallowing his saliva and he seemed oblivious of his wet chin.

From an early age he has had a knack of focusing on what people are thinking but not necessarily wanting to talk about. He is very telepathic and this was often demonstrated to us. On one clearly remembered occasion my iron pills caught my eye at the back of a cupboard. I had not thought about them for a good six months and was just wondering in my head if I should start taking them again. Tom, who was at the other end of the room and unable to see into the cupboard, said, 'Mum, I think you should take your iron pills.' It would seem that the ability to pick up other people's thoughts, far from being a useful tool in his life, merely adds to its confusion. Is he thinking his own thoughts or someone else's? It also has an amusing side. There were many occasions when we would be sitting and talking with new acquaintances. Questions would wander through our minds but be dismissed as inappropriate to bring up. In the next moment, Tom would be asking, 'Do you share a bed?' 'Are you planning to get married?' Similar thoughts to our own but even more direct!

Tom's enthusiasm and curiosity added to our exhaustion. As soon as he sorted out his speech, he took to talking to anyone and everyone he met. He would prefer to engage in conversation even if it meant wetting his pants, as he hated to miss the chance to talk to someone. Going out for a walk could take hours as he would stop and chat to every passing friend or stranger. You needed to be on your guard as, for example, after a friendly chat with one old lady he rushed forward and lifted her skirt to check whether she had any knickers on! Suddenly he would see something across the road and dash over, oblivious of the traffic, long after the age when reins might have been appropriate. He kept us on our toes by day and from our sleep by night.

St Vincent's only took children from four to seven years old, so by 1985 a decision had to be made on where he should go next. It wasn't easy to decide because Tom gave out such confusing messages about his abilities. When his IQ was tested, both by the local educational psychologist and by private practitioners, the results varied considerably depending on his own ability to concentrate that day and the tester's ability to relate to him. He invariably scored higher when the tester liked and valued him. One psychologist wrote of him as a six-year-old: 'Although I found him highly distractable, restless and impulsive, I was able to settle him to most of the tasks, although towards the end of the session it was necessary to offer the occasional climb up the wall bars as a reward for his efforts! Looking through the file, I note that Thomas has always proved difficult to assess, because of his over-activity, and the performance I witnessed does indicate a significant improvement in his attention and concentration.'

Throughout his life Tom has had the ability to surprise us. Aged five, when IQ tests were giving low and depressing indications, Tom came into our bedroom one morning and took us aback completely by reciting, nearly word-perfect, the Shakespeare poem which begins, 'When icicles hang by the wall and Dick the shepherd blows his nail . . .' He had heard his sister trying to learn it for her English homework. It was near to Christmas and he was able to surprise and amaze my family on Christmas Day by reciting it again. Despite soon forgetting it, he had given us new food for thought.

In fact, Tom's memory and verbal abilities have consistently masked his much more deep-rooted and complex problems and definitely hindered his correct school placements. Reading back over the reports he received at the age of seven shows all the 'experts' suggesting he needed to return to mainstream education with particular help focusing on his behaviour.

So started the next round of school visits, never easy as Tom could sense the tension and reacted accordingly. The local primary school wanted to take him, probably because he would be eligible for a welfare assistant, which is always a welcome addition to a class, but did not have a suitable teacher for his set. The headmistress took the trouble to ring around other heads but none could fit him in.

The Education Authority then hovered between two local special schools, one for children with moderate learning difficulties (MLD) and one for bright pupils with behaviour problems. It was felt that he didn't really fit either but that he would be better stimulated by the brighter children. We liked the teachers and the setting of the school in a large house with plenty of grounds, in the hills just outside the town. Tom was taxied to school each day and went there for the next six years. It was not the right place for him to be.

Five

Helping hands

It took five years to realise how wrong the school was for Tom. Five years during which we were not sitting still. We continued to search for a diagnosis and, we hoped, a cure. Tom seemed happy enough in the school, especially the primary section. The classes were small with around ten or twelve children and he was clearly loved by each of his form teachers. He could do a great take-off of the headmaster, catching his voice exactly, and was popular with the children in his class and protected by them outside the class.

He needed that protection, as there was a lot of bullying from the older children. Each day he would be collected by his taxi, in which were already crammed four other lads with behaviour difficulties. The driver was uninspiring but did his job. Every so often Tom would complain about the boys and show me a row of little bruises, where they had poked at him with their fingers, and I would ring the headmaster with the result that things would calm down again. It never seemed so bad that I should take on the commitment of driving and collecting him every day, which would have been very impractical as we could not afford a second car. That, at least, was the excuse I gave myself. In fact the truth is more likely that going by taxi meant that he was picked up earlier and returned later than if I had driven him and gave us a little extra time without him — a reflection of our sense of desperation. Eventually, six years later, it was one of these same boys from his taxi who jolted us into moving Tom to his next school and I still cringe at the thought of what he went through for all those years. Talking to him about it now, another six years onwards, when we are all able to review the situation from a distance, Tom says, 'I was too scared to tell you. It was my vulnerable point because he might have said I'd grassed on him. He got me back for it when you rang the Head. That was why I didn't go out from the school for playtime, because I was scared that he would beat me up. The other children were all right in my class. They didn't beat me up. Actually some of the children were OK; it was just the one boy and his brother who travelled in the taxi. I hurt, they really hurt me, not physically so much as I hurt inside.'

I know Tom is not the only child to be bullied and unable to tell his parents for fear of retribution. This is what allows bullying to persist. It just feels so sad that he didn't realise that if we had known the full extent of his unhappiness, we would have done something much sooner. Certainly none of the teachers saw this area as a problem either. It may be that he was telling us and we couldn't hear him because we didn't have an answer. We were already trying to move him to a different school for academic reasons and having no success in finding one.

The teaching at the school was adequate for most of the pupils. Tom was such a lively talker and had a great store of general knowledge in his head, gained from the constant flow of foreign visitors to our house and the conversations that went on with and around him at home. Most of the children at school, although bright, came from very limited home backgrounds which resulted in Tom being thought more intelligent than they were but this masked the underlying problems he was having with his school work. His handwriting and reading were making very slow progress and maths was far from straightforward, but there were moments, especially when a teacher had time to take down dictation for him, when we were given glimpses of the gentle, more sensitive side to his character which was usually hidden by the rush and bustle of his approach to life. Here are two poems by him which I have kept and treasured because at the time they were written they completely surprised us and gave us hope.

What is White?

White is Father Christmas' beard.
It is Beatrice's rug, soft and delicate.
It is the feathers on seagulls.
It is rice not cooked.

On a cliff

Looking down
I can hear sea gulls
Calling to their females
White as the white clouds
Up in the sky.
I can see a boat,
A big carrier boat.
It is far away
On the green sea,
Little dwarves talking to each other.
I can hear the wind sounds softly
Blowing my hair gently
It feels like ants tickling my hair
And I feel I'm in paradise.

In retrospect we may be able to see how wrong the school was for Tom and how much damage it was doing to him which, while his behaviour was fine in class, was reflected in the increasing difficulties we were having at home. With us he felt safe enough to act out his general frustration and anger with his situation. He constantly demanded our attention by incessant questions and talking and, if these were ignored or our ability to listen exhausted, he would turn to more negative attention-seeking behaviour, such as stabbing the television sound box or accidents in his pants. However, during this time we were given some very positive areas of help.

First, there was my mother who, as I have already said, did not find Tom an easy grandchild. As at that time she had another fifteen grandchildren with whom to spend her time, she could easily have seen as little of him as most of the rest of my family have done, my sister Mary being the exception. Instead she started to have Tom to stay for a night a month. She probably had no idea of the size of this gift to us and to Beatrice. It meant that for one night we could relax and sleep deeply and recharge our worn-out batteries and also give Beatrice some uninterrupted and individual time.

Another important person in our journey with Tom has been Fiona. She is a friend who lives in our town and whom we met shortly after leaving Scotland. Through good times and bad, she has been there for us and offered support and encouragement to all the family. This has been both in practical ways such as helping Tom with his reading and inviting him to meals, which he helps cook, and on an emotional and spiritual level, through counselling and meditating together. And she has not allowed Beatrice to be forgotten.

Thirdly, there was the Special Adventure Playground, a real life-saver at times. As with the playgroup in Scotland, this had been started by an individual who saw the need and set it up and we were extremely lucky to have it in the area. She persuaded the Local Authority to supply the land in the grounds of Tom's special school just outside the town. There was a large wooden building in the centre with a sizeable indoor play space and a kitchen, quiet room, cloakrooms, including showers, and an office. Outside there was a lot of wonderful, large but safe apparatus including a long slide, wide enough for three people to whiz down together, a tyre suspended on a rope which travelled along a cable and, best of all for Tom, a real fire-engine. Tom spent many happy hours in the latter and parents were encouraged to play on all the equipment as well.

We were introduced to the Adventure Playground by St Vincent's School, who took each class there once a week. It was opened by Princess Diana shortly after her marriage, and we proudly heard Tom being quoted on the national television news. 'A small boy commented that she was very brown. "Yes, but it is fading fast," replied the princess.' The

Henrietta with Tom at his christening

Nick and Tom

With Beatrice 1979

Findhorn 1981

Erraid 1979

Tom with Nick's father 1980

Findhorn 1980

Beatrice and Tom 1983

With Granny Rose 1982

Tom the prep school boy 1982

Tom at playgroup, Christmas 1981

Tom the Cub 1988

Tom the rider 1988

Henrietta and Tom house-sitting in Sussex 1990

Tom and Henrietta's mother

Tom 1984

Making a stool 1994

1995

Tom in Egypt 1996

Leaving St. John's 1997

Tom in Kenya 1997

playground, like my mother, became a strong prop to our survival during those early years. Most weekends we would go there so that Tom could let off steam. There were very supportive staff members and we met other parents who gave us the hidden information about benefits available to us. I say 'hidden' because no official source ever mentioned them to us and it was only through another mother that we learnt about such government funding as the Attendance Allowance.

When Tom moved to the special school positioned above the playground and I became a parent-governor, I discovered the political hassles the Adventure Playground had to suffer, mostly it seemed because it had been started by an inspired individual, not through the 'proper' system. It was considered an eyesore with its old boats and fire-engines, but I hope I was sometimes heard as I stressed what an essential and valuable part of our lives it was. We desperately needed breaks from Tom and this need made us feel guilty. As Tom grew older he would spend whole days without me at the centre in the holidays and knowing that he was in safe and loving hands, enjoying himself, reduced the guilt we felt about making him go there. At a time when we were finding it hard to value and love our son, it helped to see him appreciated by others. Through their eyes we could see him better.

A further benefit given us by the Playground was the chance for all of our family, including Beatrice, to meet and play with other disabled children and young adults. Able-bodied siblings were encouraged to come and take part as well and Beatrice got to know the sort of children who were hidden away when I was young. The only ones I can recall from my childhood are one friend who attended Girl Guides, whose legs had been paralysed by polio, and a neighbour's daughter who couldn't speak and disappeared into an institution before I really understood the situation. Beatrice, on the other hand, as a result of having a disabled brother, has a far better understanding of disability than Nick or I had at the same age and much less of the fear of disability that we carried into our life with Tom.

Tom's disabilities have introduced us to a number of dedicated and caring voluntary workers. Riding For the Disabled is run by volunteers and gives immense joy and pleasure to many youngsters. Again, we met this organisation through St Vincent's, who took Tom riding there once a week. The local centre is housed in the grounds of the town's racecourse and has a large indoor school and stables for the horses. During the week, sessions are held for children from nearby schools for the disabled and unemployed adults. When Tom moved schools at the age of seven, riding was not included on the curriculum but he was able to join a Sunday morning class. He loved it, and despite his inability to take part in most sports due to his lack of coordination, he became a good rider. He even won a prize in a local horse show in a class for disabled riders and was presented with a shield by Lord Oaksey, a retired jockey and racing journalist. This was a moment of great pride for his parents, which must have been similar to that experienced by my mother at school sports days when her very able children won the sack race yet again.

Most of the Riding For the Disabled took place in the indoor school, with helpers on either side of the pony and someone else leading it round and round in a circle. As Tom's riding improved, he found this rather boring . I was explaining his problem to a horse-owning acquaintance one day and she suggested that Tom have lessons on their horses from the groom that they employed. This worked well for some time, building both his confidence and his skills in riding until, just when Tom was going through his unhappiest period, he used some foul language to a passing neighbour of the friends and the lessons were withdrawn. Despite this embarrassing hiccup, Tom has continued to enjoy riding when he has the opportunity. Riding For the Disabled introduced him to a physical activity that he was able to master and take pride in and I thank the dedicated volunteers who gave up their time for him and many others.

Another caring group of volunteers who affected our lives at that time were the local Cub leaders. Tom joined the Cubs at seven years old and, despite his difficulties, was always made welcome and was helped to fit in with the group. He won a few badges, went to camp and even became a sixer. There was one funny occasion when the troop was doing a sponsored silence. At home at that time Tom was unable to stay silent for more than a moment and we could never take him somewhere where he needed to be quiet. As a result I persuaded all my friends to sponsor him for vast sums per minute, never guessing what the power of peer group pressure could achieve. I was astounded to discover, when I came to collect him, that he had managed seventy-six silent minutes. At first he had made a few grunts but when he realised that the other boys were keeping totally silent, he settled down with a toy and copied them. Eventually he did give up a little while before the others but only after he had run up large bills in sponsorship money for all my friends!

The Cub leaders have remained friends of his to this day but problems arose when he moved into the Scouts. Cubs are supervised at all times and helped in every activity. Scouts are expected to have a level of maturity that Tom had not reached and when one evening we met him by chance in the dark, miles behind the other boys and wandering down the middle of a main road, we began to worry and simultaneously Tom stopped wanting to attend.

It was, in fact, the transition between primary school and middle school at about eleven years old that Tom found very hard. Much less is expected of a primary-aged child and there is much more help on offer. It was when he reached this critical point that his frustration increased and his behaviour at home became worse. He still needed the individual help offered by the staff during his early years at school but he was no longer getting it and gradually it was recognised how little he could achieve on his own.

We were still searching for greater understanding of Tom

and help for him. Some tests suggested he was severely dyslexic, a condition which we were told at that time by our Local Education Authority only existed in the minds of middle-class, neurotic parents. The school doctor, who was also middle-class and had a daughter in the same form as Beatrice in a private school, encouraged us to look for a fee-paying school specialising in dyslexia. The first interview Tom had in one such school was a disaster as the headmaster could not cope with Tom fiddling with the things in his study while he was being interviewed and was unable to conceal his irritation. Although at other schools we were usually impressed by the standard of the staff and their abilities in handling Tom, this particular interview added to our level of anxiety on future occasions.

Each school interview took up time and emotional energy. Hopes were raised and dashed as first Nick and I would arrange to visit on our own to see if the school had potential, and then, excited at the prospect of having found somewhere that would address his needs, we would take Tom. We saw some excellent schools in lovely settings and with good facilities, nearly all of which we would have liked him to attend. After a number of rejections one headmaster suggested that his problems were too severe to fall into the category of dyslexia and that we should have him tested yet again by another psychologist he could recommend.

We fixed up the interview and tests at an Institute with a high reputation in the field of dyslexia and set off on a Friday afternoon for the two-hour journey towards London. Four o'clock on a Friday afternoon is not a good time to test anyone. Neither tester nor child are at their freshest. The psychologist could not deal with Tom's short attention span and the results were the lowest he ever achieved. It did, however, draw a line under our attempts to find him a place in a private dyslexia school, which we later discovered would not have been the right place for him anyway.

Six

Friends

By the time Tom reached the age of twelve, we were exhausted and desperate. I think the 'we' probably included Tom as
well as Nick and me, although we can only see this in hindsight. At school Tom's behaviour was no problem and he still
had the ability to stimulate the class on a verbal level and so
was a bonus to the teachers. It was at home that the real difficulties arose, mostly in his general behaviour which was
unpredictable and volatile.

Elfindale Avenue is an archetypal neat, quiet, suburban
road, especially pleasant in the late spring when the evenings
start to lengthen, the trees are in full blossom and the 1930s
houses have their tidy gardens in bloom. It is near our home
and we used to enjoy a walk along it. I say 'used to' because
I now find it hard to walk down the road without remembering one particular evening with Tom which demonstrates
the kind of behaviour with which we were trying to cope.

He was being more than usually irritating as we walked
along. He was between us, holding our hands, and kept
knocking our knuckles painfully together and shouting,
'Knuckles down.' Eventually we decided to give up on the
walk and turned round for home. He was incensed. He wanted to go on and when he saw that we were determined to
return, he lay on the ground and screamed and shouted. A
toddler tantrum in a twelve-year-old.

A toddler we could have scooped up and carried home.
An overweight twelve-year-old had us trapped. We would
have liked just to have left him to it, but it was impossible
as he had little sense of road safety and we knew from experience that he wouldn't have followed us immediately and
couldn't have safely crossed the roads on his own. In the
end, Nick decided to walk back and fetch the car, leaving me

to survive embarrassment and humiliation in the otherwise quiet road.

One of the passing cars seemed to slow down to get a good look at what was going on. I wished it would go away. It did, only to return a minute or two later. I vaguely recognised the people as acquaintances from Cubs. They kindly offered us a lift home. Tom was distracted from his rage. The issue was over for him and he climbed happily into the car. I joined him, embarrassed to be found in this predicament but so relieved to be off the street and appreciative of the kindness of the passers-by.

Tom was becoming increasingly isolated as he was unable to make friends. He couldn't join in the activities of his own age group, but was too large and clumsy for younger children. We invited in neighbours' children, but after a while their parents would start making excuses or even say directly that they did not want their children to play with him. We visited my friends with youngsters who were primed to help Tom to join in, but it was beyond them. On one occasion we went for a walk with one good friend and her son. He was, at first, keen to chat and run with Tom. That was until he ran away at speed. Tom couldn't keep up so threw his walking stick about ten yards and managed to hit the other lad plumb on the head. It was an entire fluke but it ended any friendship there and then.

We also tried inviting school friends to our house at the weekends or during holidays. By definition they also had problems and it was very hard work to keep both children happy and occupied at the same time and, given the limitations of the families that many of them came from, there was seldom a reciprocal invitation to Tom.

Cubs had been a success but Scouts had failed and Tom resisted all attempts to get him involved in other groups. What he needed was a group of children just like himself but we couldn't find such a group in the town His main preoccupations were, and still are, clothes, music and Dr Who. Most other children he knew wore T-shirts and jeans but Tom has never liked either of these, the former in particular because they do not have collars and so cannot be worn with a tie. Ties, for Tom, are the essential requisite for the day. For many years the tie has been the first item chosen, then the shirt to go with it. He has been known to set off down the road in nothing else! He often sleeps in a tie and on a day trip to Alton Towers Tom will be the only male out of the thousands visiting that day to wear one. It is possible to think that there is no harm in having an unusual choice of dress but in fact it further separated him from his peer group

He did actually have a group of friends, but most were octogenarians. Frieda we met as a result of a visit to a near-by National Trust property. Tom enjoys visiting castles and stately homes and we have taken him to see many, although they can be fraught occasions. He has managed to set off alarms by stumbling over the rope separating the visitors from the antiques. Each room usually has an attendant to give added information and keep an eye on things. Tom is always full of questions and asked one attendant if she had been around in Tudor times! Once she realised that he was not being rude but had no understanding of dates and years, she entered into the spirit of his enquiry and acted the part of an historical character.

On one occasion, Frieda was walking around the gardens while we were visiting with Tom, Beatrice and one of my nieces. Caroline was older but smaller than Tom and we had asked her to keep him company. She was leaning over and gazing into a fish pond when Tom could not resist the impulse to push. As we pulled her out again and others watched, Frieda hurried over and lent us her jacket in which to wrap the startled, wet and crying Caroline. I doubt if Caroline wanted further days out with us but Frieda, we discovered, was a customer at our bookshop and became a close friend to all the family and especially Tom. She had been a special needs teacher and was determined to help Tom to learn to read, giving him weekly lessons for some years. His reading didn't progress very far but they both enjoyed the classes until she herself became too old and confused and the lessons had to end.

Charles, a local retired vicar in his nineties, and his friend Kathleen also met us through our bookshop and regularly invited Tom round for vast teas, much appreciated by him. This older group of friends had time for him and enjoyed his endless chatter and his choice of clothes. The only down-side to these relationships was that they allowed him constant centre-stage. He then expected his own age group to treat him in the same way and was unable to adapt to them.

Seven

Searching

After experimenting with the hospital over possible food allergies when Tom was four years old, we had little more to do with the National Health Service apart from the normal childhood illnesses and the fairly frequent trips to the hospital when Tom had accidents due to his clumsiness. However, our search for an answer and possibly a cure continued through the alternative health route.

Our first such visit, when we moved back to England, was to a cranial osteopath. We thought that perhaps Tom's skull had been moved out of place at birth by the forceps and could be corrected by an osteopath. Tom and I set off for the clinic in the next town. We had a card with the appointment time but discovered when we reached the consulting rooms that we had been written into the book for an hour later. With a good book to read waiting an extra hour can be quite enjoyable, but trying to amuse and keep Tom quiet for that time was awful. Eventually he was seen but, in view of his need to be constantly on the move and the osteopath's inability to calm him down, he felt he could do little for him. It was a waste of time and a lot of nervous energy.

Next, a friend who practises the Alexander Technique offered to see him. His wife had been giving Tom some reading lessons so he already knew Tom well and was able to relax him and work on him. Despite having had sessions of this technique myself, I have never really understood it and do not know whether it benefited Tom. It did feel good, however, to be offered some help and attention and to think it might be making a difference. In a way those thoughts reflect our ongoing sense of isolation. I am sure other friends wanted to help but either didn't know how or were caught up in their own busy lives and didn't realise our sense of desperation at the time. I tried not to be disappointed in friends and family and I am equally sure that I have been so tied up in my own world and troubles that I have frequently failed to see the needs of others and have missed the opportunity of giving them a helping hand.

As already mentioned, we had tried two private dyslexia consultants. One recommended an optician who has a national reputation for work with children with learning difficulties and just happened to live in our town. All these practitioners and consultants are expensive, especially when you have to add in the cost of travel to far-flung places, food and time off work. It was nice to hear of someone so close by, and we took Tom along. He was already wearing strong glasses for short-sightedness so it seemed worth going down this avenue. Another long report later we learnt that the optician felt Tom's problems were non-visual and not amenable to specific vision training. He went on to add that he thought 'the variety of problems that Tom manifested would suggest a pattern of brain damage subsequent to his complex birth history' and he recommended yet another specialist, nearly four hours' drive away, as the best person to advise us next.

An appointment was made and we set off on the long drive north. Tom was by now ten years old and luckily enjoyed car journeys. From the outside the clinic looked disappointingly like a small, dull house but the greeting was friendly and the waiting room full of entertainment. As it was a centre for brain-damaged people, there was love and understanding for both Tom and ourselves and we all soon relaxed. Tom liked the doctor and did his best to slow down and work hard in the tests. As I understand it, the principle of the treatment offered is that babies are born with a set of reflexes necessary to help them survive the challenges of the first few years of life, but that as they grow up these are inhibited and adult reflexes take over. The centre believes that in brain-damaged babies often the baby reflexes are not replaced, while in adults who suffer a stroke or accident the immature reflexes will sometimes reappear and hinder progress. Further development in other areas of learning is restricted if the baby reflexes are present. Apparently the early reflexes change as the baby learns to crawl, so a treatment programme has been developed which includes long sessions, twice daily, of crawling motions and exercises.

At last it felt that someone was looking at Tom in depth in the right areas and understanding the fundamental problems he had. Every three months we made the journey back up to the centre and between visits we coaxed and persuaded Tom, at least once a day, to cooperate with the time-consuming and often boring exercises. It really needed both Nick and me to be involved in each session, especially at the beginning, and perhaps Tom cooperated so well because he was getting our undivided attention.

After a year, tests seemed to show some improvements and we were also advised to have his hair analysed for signs of mineral deficiencies in his body. It is thought that hyperactive children with behaviour problems tend to be deficient in zinc, magnesium and manganese. The results suggested a lack of these minerals in Tom, so we sent off for a large consignment of pills. The process of taking them was complicated by the fact that each type needed to be administered at a different time of the day. Both the pills and the treatment were not cheap but we felt we were doing something positive for Tom and the support we received from everyone at the centre encouraged us to continue, both with the visits and the exercises, for two and a half years. We will never know how much difference this treatment made to Tom and when we eventually received help from more orthodox medicine, the hours we had put in exercising with Tom were ignored as irrelevant. In the end we gave up this route when circumstances at school took a turn and it was no longer practicable.

We all worked hard at the exercises, Tom included, but his behaviour at home did not improve and, in fact, became increasingly difficult. He started having panic attacks. The cause of these varied and each type happened just once or twice. On one occasion he couldn't get over the threshold of his bedroom door because there was a minute moth in the room. It took about an hour to get him to bed that night. Another time he began sweating and trembling in a crowded shop as he tried to pay for goods at the till. A few times he has been completely rooted to the spot by vertigo. Once he had gone up a tower in a castle in France by himself and we stood at the bottom to wave to him. We waited and waited but he didn't appear at the top and eventually Nick climbed the spiral staircase to find him pressed against the roof unable to move and being eyed by a German couple who were wondering what was happening.

These panic attacks came and went but one developed into a real trial to us all. This related to being separated from us. He began to refuse to dress for school, which may not be unusual in children, but then he started to act in the same way for all clubs and activities he was planning to do on his own. However much he had been looking forward to an outing, when the time came he found it nearly impossible to get himself out of the house and usually I finished up in tears of rage and frustration before he would go. It was very wearing.

Another equally exhausting foible was the way he would latch on to a word or phrase which would set him off like a stuck gramophone record. If I ever used the word 'American' he would tell me for the next twenty minutes that I was saying it wrong and with an American accent. And if anybody mentioned the place 'Ironbridge', we were in for an equally long period of 'Mummy and Daddy had an argument at Ironbridge.' We were eventually helped with this when the school doctor gave the behaviour a name — 'perseveration'. After that it became easier to tolerate and we developed a way of breaking the pattern by joining in with it and exaggerating the scenario. For example, the story of the argument at Ironbridge developed into how we had tipped a policeman over the bridge as we argued and had thrown custard pies at each other! The laughter this produced would speed up the interruption of the behaviour pattern.

Even an obvious and simple occupation like going to the cinema could be a minefield. Our local cinema is an old, large Odeon converted into five new cinemas. Screen One is the original upstairs with a big screen and steeply banked seats. On one occasion, Tom rushed eagerly up the stairs right to the back, only to be frozen by vertigo when he turned round to look at the screen. It took quite a while to coax him back down the stairs to where he could relax and watch the film — all this taking place as an entertainment or distraction for the rest of the audience.

Another time, we made the mistake of taking him to the new Batman film. I feel instant tension as I start remembering the occasion. It was a film rated for twelve-year-olds and over. He was thirteen but still not really old enough for it and he found it difficult to settle into the story. He wriggled, talked and burped constantly, irritating our neighbours and making it impossible for Nick and me to enjoy it either. When he is bored, he insists on frequent visits to the lavatory. We were getting desperate, so when he got up yet again we made our plans to escape. The loo had no outside exit but we left our seats and waited for him to reappear, hiding on either side of the doorway. We managed to surprise him and hurriedly marched him to the exit. As we reached the door and he realised what was happening, the screams started and lasted all down the stairs, through the foyer and for most of the walk home. But that was better than remaining in the cinema.

By the time Tom was twelve, Nick and I were exhausted, confused and overwhelmed. We needed help but didn't know where to get it from. In the end it came from an obvious but, to us, unexpected direction. I had arranged to see the family GP. I don't remember why I was seeing him but that appointment was a turning point in the story of Tom's journey through life. It had snowed that morning. Snow always manages to take the English by surprise and the roads were still blocked and slippery so I left the car behind and walked about a mile to the doctor's surgery in my Wellington boots. I discovered when I arrived that most people had cancelled their appointments. This meant that instead of the usual five minutes with the doctor, when one struggles to be coherent under the pressure of time and a full waiting room, I knew that there was no one booked for at least forty minutes after me. At last I had time, through my tears, to explain to the doctor the confusion and pain that we were suffering and for once I really felt I had been heard by a practitioner of orthodox medicine. Immediately he referred us back to the paediatrician at the hospital whom we had not seen since Tom was about five years old.

Now things started to move. Tests were done on Tom, including a brain scan, EEGs and genetic explorations. While we waited for the results a clinical psychologist visited us and offered help regarding his behaviour. Eventually we went back to see the specialist to hear the results of the investigations. He spelt out his conclusion to his findings using a very old-fashioned and currently unpopular phrase. He told us that Tom was 'mentally retarded'. I hated this expression. It shocked us and took time and tears to digest, but it meant that we heard what he was telling us. The modern phrases such as 'learning difficulties' and 'special needs' are so wide and vague that they can mean anything and had made it easier for us to avoid the reality of Tom's situation. We had continued to hope that Tom would grow out of his difficulties and fulfil the potential that we could see he had. Now we learnt to view him all over again. This did not mean that we gave up on his potential but we recognised his current limitations. At last we were able to unburden him of the weight of our unrealistic hopes and expectations.

What became immediately obvious with this new diagnosis was that Tom was in the wrong school, a school for bright children with behaviour problems. No wonder he had been so unhappy. At first, when we spoke to the Local Education officer, we were frustrated by his saying that Tom's

Statement would be reviewed automatically when he reached the age of thirteen and that nothing could be done before then. (The educational Statement is a document originally produced on Tom when he was seven and based on a number of reports from doctors, educational psychologists and teachers. Once accepted by the Local Education Authority it commits them to supplying the agreed education and facilities.) We argued with this bureaucratic and, to our mind, unreasonable attitude. We had been worrying about the suitability of his school for some time and were not prepared to wait unnecessary months before he could be moved. With luck and persistence, after further discussion the logic of this was eventually seen and the review was brought forward.

A new series of reports and tests was initiated. Tom was seen again by the educational psychologist, who suggested an IQ between fifty and seventy and recommended a school for children with Moderate Learning Difficulties (MLD). There is one such day school in the town but we were not enthusiastic about it. It didn't help our attitude to the suggested placement that I was by now working as a probation officer and many of the young people whom I saw in my job had attended this school. Class also became an issue. We were told that there were no children in the school at that time of 'professional' parents. Most came from families where many members had been to the same school, often including the parents. They were limited children of limited families. This would make it very hard for Tom to make friends. He had a sister at a private school, doing her A levels and likely to go to university. She was about to go to China to teach during her Gap year. He needed to be at a school which included at least some other children from similar homes.

There was an MLD school in the next town which had a much better reputation. Any parents from our town with 'get up and go' had managed to send their children there. We went to have a look around it. The staff were friendly, the children looked happy and the general atmosphere was good despite the very cramped physical surroundings on a small plot of land beside a motorway. However, we were told by the headmaster, and it was repeated by the form master, that the school was completely full and had a long waiting list. In the end, when the Local Authority accepted that the local MLD school was unsuitable and knew we would appeal against a placement there, they insisted that the better school offer him a place, jumping him to the front of the queue. However, by this time we and many of the experts compiling their reports felt that Tom needed a boarding placement.

As his parents, our preference for boarding was strongly influenced by our need for a break from his constant demand on our time and attention, but this was not the motive of the doctors and psychologists who supported us. With variations, the reports from the paediatrician, county medical officer, school doctor, clinical psychologist and educational psychologist all suggested that Tom was becoming more and more socially isolated, failing to find friends either at school because of the social differences or at home because of his inability to keep pace with his peer group. It was generally felt that he would have a better opportunity to make friends in the wider social mix of a boarding school. Most of them also thought that he would take more personal responsibility for his life and control his behaviour better if he had a round-the-clock and consistent structured environment. The implication was that at home we were not strict enough with him, which was probably true, but we felt worn down with our attempts to help him conform.

We found ourselves a solicitor from the East Midlands who specialised in fighting appeals against Local Education Authority decisions on schooling. Our county had no suitable boarding places to offer in their schools and we were all aware of the cost of boarding 'out of county'. By now we felt strongly that Tom had been in the wrong school for six years and that it was essential that we find him the right place this time. It was inevitable, but a pity, that the cost of schooling rather than Tom's needs was dictating the decision that the Local Authority had come to. The opinions of most of the experts were ignored.

We had mixed feelings about boarding him. All of his male first cousins attended expensive private boarding schools, as their parents thought this was the best they could do for them. The difference for us was the confusion created by our own need for a break from Tom. Were we trying to send him away from home because we couldn't cope and because we wanted a chance to enjoy our lives? These were not comfortable questions and would have been easier to deal with if we had been given the support of our Education Authority to look at the complete picture. Instead we had to repress these anxieties and argue the case for boarding, when in fact the basis of the Authority' argument was financial, although this was left unspoken. Tom, too, had very mixed feelings. He didn't want to leave home but was very keen to change schools. He seemed to accept that there were no suitable local schools so he would have to go away.

The wheels of bureaucracy move very slowly. First, our solicitor came with us to a meeting with the Education Officer involved. He was sympathetic to our position and if he had held the power to decide would probably have agreed to our choice of boarding school straight away. We had discovered an extraordinary private special school for children with moderate and severe learning difficulties. Perhaps it should be called unique. It was in a wonderful setting in the country, with plenty of grounds and a long drive that culminated in a circular sweep to a large Georgian house with a pillared porch more suitable for a horse-drawn carriage than a car. It was part of the large estate belonging to a Lord and was rented to the school. As it was full of beautiful antiques and flower arrangements, it was easy to mistake it for a National Trust property. The headmistress was a real character. She, her desk and the school dog were all vast She always seemed to be seated behind her large desk, with her tall, thin sister standing beside her. When she met Tom, wearing his bow tie for the interview, she assured us he would fit in. 'He's an eccentric and we are all eccentrics here.' It was the first time we had heard him valued for his oddities and we knew that at this school he would not be a square peg pushed into a round hole. He could be himself. The Education Officer also recognised this when he visited the school but had no choice, due to county policy, but to reject the place.

The next step was a local Appeal in the county town. Again the solicitor came with us. We had already sent in all our supporting evidence including a long letter from us as Tom's parents. The Appeal was held in a large impersonal room in the Shire Hall and, despite the good body of opinion supporting our choice of school, it was almost inevitable that we would lose because of the financial constraints on the county. We had to wait a while to hear the decision but, as expected, we did lose, so we took our case to the Secretary of State for Education and that seemed to take for ever. We had started asking for a review of Tom's Statement when he was twelve and he was very nearly sixteen and due to leave school before we eventually won our Appeal.

In the meantime, fate took a hand in the process. I was sitting one day in the Youth Court in my role as a probation officer when the young lad who had travelled in Tom's taxi for the past six years, and who I knew had bullied him from time to time, appeared in the dock on an assault charge. It had been a nasty attack and I suddenly knew, there and then, that we could not let Tom continue attending that school or travelling in that taxi. We would find the money to pay his fees while the appeal system continued. We knew the costs would not be backdated, even if we were successful in our appeal, but it felt really right to make the move. Special schools are even more expensive than ordinary private schools but with help from my mother, my sister-in-law and an increased mortgage we managed to pay the fees for the two and a half more years that it took to win the appeal.

With hindsight we can see that when Tom moved to his new school at the age of thirteen we had passed the lowest point in his childhood. Since then, for all of us, life has steadily improved. Around this time the paediatrician decided that Tom's short, sharp regular headaches were a mild form of epilepsy and prescribed the drug Tegratol. The doctor thinks that this made all the difference. It certainly made him sleepy and reduced the head cramps but the latter could have been caused by the stress and pressure of being in the wrong school. Whatever the reason, Tom relaxed and started to blossom.

Some pupils in the new school were paid for by their Local Authority and some by their parents and we had found the mixture of children for which we had hoped. Tom started making friends and being invited out by other visiting families. There was a high expectation on behaviour in the school but no bullying. For the first time in thirteen years Tom stopped wetting the bed. Plenty of sport was played and the school had its own farm and horses, and Tom, who was quite fat by now, started losing weight and was a less compulsive eater at home. He still couldn't read, write or use numbers but at least he was happier.

The effect of the boarding arrangement on Nick and myself was no less profound than on Tom. For the first few weeks we found it nearly impossible to get out of bed at the weekends. Beatrice often gave us breakfast in bed on a Saturday, before leaving for school, and there we would stay! For so long we had been forced to leap up on Saturdays and Sundays to entertain Tom. He always needed a good long walk in an attempt to use up his seemingly inexhaustible energy. It took a couple of months to find our own reasons for getting going and then we both experienced a flood of energy into our systems that we had forgotten we possessed. The house and garden shone and Beatrice must have had more attention from us than we had given her for years.

The next significant day for me in Tom's life was 28th February, 1993. This was the date of his confirmation. He had been christened as a baby, not because we were regular churchgoers and needed him accepted into the Church of England, but because we believed in the importance of our spiritual lives and wanted to recognise and celebrate this aspect of him. In fact Tom enjoys church services and when he was offered the chance of confirmation classes at school was keen to go through this process. Various friends and members of our family came with us to his confirmation. It was a moving service, seeing these youngsters take part who all had their own challenges in life. Tom was delighted to be able to receive communion for the first time and told the bishop afterwards that he thought the wine was a very good vintage! In the village there was an excellent restaurant, the kind that we would not normally have taken Tom into because of his problems in conforming to expected standards of behaviour. However the school had suggested that we eat there as other families, down for their child's confirmation, would do the same. We had a great meal. Three similar groups took up the whole restaurant. Tom chose venison. He loves to try out dishes which he has never eaten before and makes a refreshing change from 'fish fingers and peas only' children. One boy from another table kept coming over to talk to us and show us the Bible he had been given, so if Tom needed to get up and wander around it did not matter.

It was a really successful day. A happy, family day. The sort that had been so few and far between in his life. Throughout the day I had this strong sense that Tom had at last come fully into his physical body. It was as if at birth his spirit had not quite made it into this dimension and as a result his brain could not fully control his physical body. I am not suggesting that there was a magic cure for all his ills on that day but subsequently he always felt different to me. It may well be that I had been able to relax with him that day and so was able to value him more.

About a month later, during the school holidays, Tom spent the day with Celia, a friend of ours, whose own children had already grown up. It was a rare occasion for him to be invited out like this and he was nervous about going, so we had to help him through the inevitable panic attack, but eventually he went. Afterwards she wrote to us and I have kept the letter because at the time it reduced me to tears, while also managing to introduce us to aspects of Tom's character that, up to then, we had completely missed.

Dear Henrietta and Nick,
I feel I want to write to you just to say what good company Tommy was the other day. (We'll do it again.) I'm sure he was on his best behaviour — in fact he said he was! So I got the full benefit of his generous and open nature — and I was terribly impressed by his wide knowledge and use of language and lovely sense of humour — we had lots of laughs . . .
. . . and very aware of what a tremendous task you have with him and how imaginatively and lovingly you do it all. Have a lovely Easter time in Sussex.
With love, Celia

I can honestly say that until we received that letter I had never noticed his sense of humour or his generous nature. I was always so busy telling him to close his mouth when he ate, do up his flies, be quiet, blow his nose etc, etc, that I had missed the much more delightful and essential aspects of his character. I am so grateful to Celia because since then I too have been able to enjoy his funny side. It was also good to hear us being appreciated as parents. I expect others have said similar things but it is easy to miss it when it is not written down.

Tom attended his boarding school in Dorset for two and a half years. Initially it was definitely the right school for him. As always he was liked and valued by the staff but this time even his eccentricities were valued With no bullying he was able to relax. The academic standard of the school was not high nor, we began to realise, were the teachers experts in dealing with special needs, but the relaxed and happy atmosphere allowed Tom to gain confidence in himself and recover from the stress of his previous school.

After more expert reports, updating letters from ourselves and long phone calls with both our solicitor and the Ministry of Education, we eventually won our Appeal and it was agreed that Tom should be boarding. He already had been for over two years and was due to leave school the following term, aged sixteen. In view of this, and because the fees could not be backdated, the Secretary of State for Education decided that Tom should board for a further three years. Coincidentally the school we had sent him to had been de-registered by the Ministry, so the county could not consider paying for him to stay there and suddenly we were searching for a new placement for him.

Boarding schools for over-sixteens that are approved by the Ministry are few and far between. We were given suggestions of schools in West Wales, Yorkshire and Brighton. By now both Nick and I had full-time jobs while Tom was still in Dorset, so visiting these schools was logistically challenging! Luckily we realised quite quickly, after visiting two Steiner schools and a local agricultural college, all set in the depths of the country, that Tom is not a rural creature and that he would be far happier in a town setting. We had spent many happy holidays in Sussex, so organised a visit to St John's School in Brighton. Although the physical conditions — a red brick school crammed on the side of a steep hill — lacked the beauty and spaciousness of his Dorset school, we quickly realised that the level of teaching was far higher, as was the expectation of Tom's potential achievement. The past three years in Dorset had helped him regain some of his confidence. Now he was ready to start learning again.

Eight
Spiritual healers

Orthodox medical doctors, practitioners of alternative medicine and educational specialists were some of the experts
we visited during our endless search for help with Tom —
help with both a diagnosis and a cure. Another group that
cannot be forgotten were the spiritual healers. Nick, who has
always been interested in healing, was in the early years of
our marriage assisting and learning from a healer called
Christa. Despite my scepticism, when I was trying to con-
ceive a child and before starting on fertility tests at the hospital, I went to see her for help with getting pregnant.

Seven years previously I had damaged my knee in a skiing accident. I had travelled all the way out to Switzerland
for a long weekend of skiing and fell on the first run. I was
so keen to keep on skiing that I was stupid enough to let the
doctor strap up my leg and inject it with a pain killer, after
he had told me that I had torn a ligament in the knee. As a
result, I had a wonderful time on the slopes and regretted it
every time I turned over in bed for the next seven years.

When I went in to see Christa for the first time, she knew
nothing about my knee. She says she can see an energy field
around the body and works by directing power through her
body, holding her hands a number of feet from the patient
but pointed at the troublesome area. As soon as I sat down
she told me that she could see a scar in the energy field
around my knee and she rubbed her fingers in the air about
a yard from my leg. The outcome was that I have never had
pain in that knee since then and it gave me a lot of confidence in her powers as a healer.

By the time we had moved south and Tom was four,
Christa had married her healer teacher. After Tom's failed
placement in the private primary school we decided to ask

for their help. It was a three-hour car journey to Kent and, after seeing him, they told us he had severe problems that would need a lot of treatment if they were going to be able to help him. We didn't go again. We told ourselves that it was too far to go on a regular basis but I think the real reason was that we were not ready to hear the truth about the seriousness of his condition. We were still hoping he would grow out of his difficulties and had hoped for a miracle cure in one visit.

My mother attends a Christian Science church and her religion has been a part of my upbringing. Although I have never fully committed myself to this path, at times I have been drawn to the church services. Healing plays a central part in Christian Science, with the belief that we are the perfect reflections of God and that the Divine Mind has the power to heal the material body. While Tom attended a day school and lived near his grandmother, we often went with her to church. All Christian Science churches have a Sunday School for youngsters up to the age of twenty, which takes place at the same time as the adult service. When they had a suitable teacher who could cope with Tom, I would go to the church service while Beatrice and Tom went to the Sunday School. My motives were twofold. First, it would give me a quiet hour without the children, although I could never quite relax as my ears would be listening out for sounds of Tom. Second, I was always hoping that 'a healing' would take place. I know that my mother, despite gloomy medical diagnoses and Tom's ability to irritate, has always held on to her love for him and has tried to see him 'as he really is, perfect as his Father in Heaven is perfect'.

A few years on from the trip to Christa, Nick again became involved with a healer. This time it was a man, Edward, who practised locally, or at least only about thirty miles away. I am not sure that I ever met him. I had been disappointed by our trip to Christa and left Nick to take Tom to this new healer if he wanted to. In fact they went for a few weeks and Edward would hold his hands over Tom for about half an hour or as long as Tom could be persuaded to stay still. They even took the tortoise with a damaged leg along with them once. I never felt these visits made any difference. The tortoise died and we gave up on spiritual healers for a while.

Tom was twelve when we made our third and final attempt to achieve a miracle healing. This was during the most difficult period of Tom's childhood, when we were definitely ready to grasp at straws. We were running our bookshop at the time and Nick came across a booklet about a healer in Wales who according to the histories of those who had visited him was a very special person with extraordinary powers. Why not have another go? The result would be so wonderful and if we didn't see him we would always wonder what might have been. So again we allowed ourselves to build up our hopes and arranged yet another four-hour journey. We booked to see him at a weekend and organised accommodation at a farmhouse Bed and Breakfast through the tourist office in Machynlleth.

The drive was beautiful, as was the setting of the healer's home down a long wooded and winding drive. We were shown into a shed in the garden and waited. Eventually a much younger man than we expected arrived and told us that his father was not able to see Tom but that he, the son, would do his best to help. It could be said that we didn't have the faith in the son to let him do the healing, or that faith healers do not work. There could be numerous reasons why no miracle took place depending on one's belief system. From where I am now, I would suggest that we hadn't yet understood the purpose of our relationship with Tom or gained from the lessons he was offering us. It took another six years of growth and change by us all before Tom spelt out very clearly why he was with us.

The healing we had hoped for may not have happened that weekend but we certainly gained from the trip. We stayed for the two nights with a delightful farming family. When Tom was twelve we were still finding it hard to see his strengths buried under his difficult and demanding behaviour but the family saw them and so enjoyed his company that the mother and daughter wrote to him the following week. Again I kept the note, as viewing Tom through the eyes of others helped us to see him more clearly.

Dear Tommy,
Just a little note from Wales! We were thinking of you yesterday and do hope that you enjoyed seeing Harlech Castle. After you had gone I did all the washing and cleaning and then I made lunch. In the afternoon I had a little sit in the sun before it was time to take Gilly back to school. We loved having you to stay — hope your Welsh flag is up in your bedroom.
Love and hugs from us all,
Susan and Gilly

Tom's openness of heart and enthusiasm for life means that he can touch people in a wonderful way. I doubt if our hosts wrote to many of their numerous guests after they left and this note, like Celia's, acted as a beacon for us in our darker times. Nick and I stayed with Susan again recently. Six years later she still remembered Tom well. She told us that it was his eccentricity that had appealed to her. She continued to carry a clear image of him leaving in the car to visit Harlech Castle, wearing a waistcoat and bow tie and waving his Welsh flag while singing 'Men of Harlech'!

Nine

Family holidays

We took Tom on his first holiday when he was six weeks old. During the pregnancy we had decided to travel soon after his birth to the Lot Valley in France to stay with French friends in their old converted farmhouse. The idea behind the trip was that it was easier to travel with a very small, breast-fed baby than with a toddler. I had not by then learnt to release plans that any sensible person could see were bound to fail.

I have already described my lack of milk and Tom's constant cries of hunger. The birth had been nearly a month later than originally expected and I hadn't fully recovered from the Caesarean operation. Tom slept with us in a pram between our beds. Beatrice slept next door and our friends in the room above. While the walls of the old farmhouse were so thick that we needed a baby alarm to hear Beatrice in the next room, our ceiling consisted of the wood of our hosts' bedroom floor, with large gaps between the boards. My memory of the holiday is of sleepless nights as I constantly rocked the pram to stop Tom's cries being heard above us. After that holiday we limited our trips from Findhorn to visits to the grandparents!

With Tom aged four, and about to start at a mainstream school, we risked another trip to France. This time we went camping with English friends near Avignon. It nearly matched up to my dream family holiday. Tom was already usually very active but just before we set off he had a really heavy dose of flu, running a high temperature for a week. Both children slept all night as we drove down through France. For Beatrice this was not surprising as she has always been a deep sleeper but for Tom it was very unusual. When we reached the campsite he sat and watched us putting up the tent. He was a changed child, sitting gazing into space most of the time and sleeping well at night. What bliss! We could sit around the camp fire and chat with our friends and Beatrice played happily with the other children. The bliss lasted about two days. Tom continued being exhausted and Nick and I joined him. We both had high temperatures for a week — not a pleasure in a dusty campsite in a heatwave. We all three just about recovered in time to go home! I'm glad to say Beatrice had a good holiday with our friends but it cured us again for quite a few years of the urge for long-distance travels.

We then found a role as house-sitters for other families off on holiday. Isolated houses preferably, so that we could relax away from contact with other people who might react to Tom's behaviour. For two years we went to Shropshire, where the argument at Ironbridge took place, which was to haunt us for the next few years. Another memory, apart from the rain and the walks on the Long Mynd, is of my punish-ment for swearing. Tom had been picking up some awful language at school and had a rich vocabulary of swear words, mostly four-letter ones. In our attempt to halt the flow we had decided that if he swore during the day he would have no pudding for supper. We went for yet anoth-er wet walk and I lost my temper and was heard to say, 'You can go bloody anywhere.' That evening we had some beau-tiful, fat, fresh yellow pears which I can still see so clearly in my head and which I had to watch the others eat. The inci-dent certainly cured me of my very moderate habit of swear-ing and Tom has never let me forget the misdemeanour. I think my punishment and the fact that I suffered it without question also helped him to control his language.

House-sitting was the very opposite of shared family hol-idays but we have had many wonderful trips to Ditchling in Sussex. The friends have dogs, cats, house plants and a greenhouse that need looking after. We, in return, have use of their beautiful home with a vast garden, field, swimming pool, tennis court and a playroom full of toys, with no close neighbours to be disturbed and room for other family members to join us for odd days.

As Tom settled in boarding school and gained a modicum more control over himself, we tried another holiday to France. Friends again lent us a house, this time in the Loire valley — a beautiful, isolated old French farmhouse down a long grassy track. Beatrice came the first time but then started to travel without us. Nick, Tom and I discovered the joys of bicycling in France. Tom wobbles too much to be safe on the busy English roads, but down quiet country lanes in France there are so few cars that it is possible to stop and pull over if one does appear.

Tom cannot read a book but is still very well read thanks to both tapes and the fact that Nick is an excellent reader. On holiday, Tom and I will cut out and stick models while Nick entertains us with such stories as *Gulliver's Travels*, *Twenty Thousand Leagues Under the Sea* and *Just William*.

Beatrice has been on many holidays without us, starting with school trips, trips with aunts and then with friends. Tom is fascinated by the world and loves to travel but still needs support to do so. He has difficulty understanding British money as number has so little meaning for him, so foreign money is even more impossible. He can learn facts about money. For example, he learnt over the years that a double Dr Who video costs £19.99 but if he had a £20 note he would panic about whether he had enough. He eventually learnt that it was enough and that he would get a penny change but then he would be equally confused if he had £25 in his hand. Add to this price changes and the fact that he is shy to admit his problem to the salesperson and it is possible to see the handicap he faces in life arising from this aspect of number alone. Time, size, sequence and pattern are all a mystery to him as well.

Before Tom started boarding, Nick and I solved the problem of our need for time off from looking after him by taking separate holidays. We took it in turns to go on interesting and relaxing trips but we were delighted when the first opportunity came for us to have a holiday together alone. Tom was too much for my mother to manage on her own for more than a night or two but when he was about nine the school took him away for four nights. Beatrice was very happy to board at her school and Nick and I booked in to see friends. We were so keen to see as many people as possible that we underestimated the distances between them and finished up spending most of the four days travelling in the car, but the break still did us good. We also learnt from our mistakes and the following year, when the same opportunity arose, we persuaded my mother to look after Tom for the weekend, with the help of Beatrice, and thus made the four nights into a week. At the time we were running our mail-order bookshop from our home and a kind customer, to whom we had chatted over the phone for some years but never met in person, invited us to stay in the south of France. Once there we hardly moved. It was a really blissful, restful week that felt like at least a month.

In 1995 we decided that Tom's behaviour had improved so much that we would book a package holiday to Austria. He had always wanted to visit Germany but was fascinated by the war and we were still nervous of what he might come out with in conversation, so Austria was his second choice.

We stayed in Westendorf, a ski resort in winter and a centre for walkers in the summer. We kept ourselves well exercised up the mountains and Tom practised his yodelling with enthusiasm. He was in his element. He loves music and the village was full of it: a brass band in the central square, a zither in the pub, yodelling lessons in a hut up the mountain. Wearing shorts and his new Austrian hat and tie, and holding his walking stick, he strode with us over the hills. Just as we reached exhaustion point, there was always a chalet serving beer and vast lunches to tuck into.

Although the village was packed with visitors, there were few children staying there and the only other boy in our hotel also had learning difficulties. This helped to relax us. For some reason most of the guests were Scottish and all were friendly. We shared our dinner table for the two weeks with a Scottish couple who showed their enjoyment of Tom's company by writing him limericks.

> *There was a young man called Tom.*
> *He came into our lives like a bomb.*
> *Ein Raddler Bier*
> *Set him off in top gear*
> *And he'd yodel all the way home!*

> *There was a young man called Tom Rose*
> *Who was handsome and liked stylish clothes.*
> *New hat, knife and tie*
> *Really cheered up this guy*
> *Next year — lederhosen? Who knows?*

They also sent him a tape of Scottish music on their return home and a second couple sent him the cassette version of War of the Worlds. Tom has this ability to enter people's hearts, which becomes more obvious to us as he gets older.

The only low point of the holiday was when we reached Gatwick on the return journey to discover that he had left three hats behind in a carrier bag on a chair in Salzburg airport, including his new Austrian one complete with feathered brooch. He realised while we waited in the luggage hall and was heartbroken — and everyone around knew it. The difference with most of us is that we would have been upset but would have tried to hide this fact from all but our closest friends and then regretted the loss for years. Tom, on the other hand, expresses his feelings in the moment at full volume and then it is over for him. It is a simple and effective way of dealing with distress but quite overwhelming at the time for those around him.

Austria had been a success, but very expensive, so the next year we tried another package holiday — this time to Luxor, Egypt. It was a surprisingly cheap holiday and an even greater success. Four of us travelled: Nick, myself, Tom and his godmother, Annabel. She wanted the chance to get to know Tom better. We knew we only had six days in Egypt and hoped to experience the country and the local people, so we chose to stay in one town rather than travel around, and in a hotel in the centre instead of one of the usual package hotels on the outskirts of the town, which were surrounded by beautiful gardens to cushion the tourists from the locals.

Even without Tom it would have been a good holiday, but with him it was a great experience. Tom talks to everyone he meets and soon made good friends with the hotel staff, the head waiter in particular. They found an affinity in clothes. I have already described Tom's love of ties, even choosing one to wear in bed at night. By the end of the holiday they had exchanged ties.

Tom likes to try new dishes on the menu and was keen to eat Egyptian food. When he made this known, the manager insisted on serving us an Egyptian meal rather than the European buffet produced for the other tourists.

Having Tom with us literally opened doors. One night we went to another restaurant. Stuffed pigeon was on the menu and, never having tasted it, Tom chose it. Alas, it was not available that night. The head waiter of this restaurant could see his disappointment and invited us to come to his home two nights later, where his wife would cook the dish. We waited outside our hotel at the appointed time and wondered if he would arrive. He did, and took us by taxi to his village where he lived with his wife and three children.

First we were shown around the house. As it never rains in Luxor, the village houses are built of mud bricks and on the flat roof were chickens and rabbits. The wife and children ate in one room while the husband entertained the four of us. Tom had his stuffed pigeon and the rest of us ate lamb. It was the last night of Ramadan (the month in which Muslims fast between sunrise and sunset) so we had to sit and watch our food until the cannon was fired in Luxor to tell people Ramadan was over. The meal was delicious. It was a memorable evening and a real experience of Egyptian Egypt.

Although Tom looks like any eighteen-year-old lad, people soon realise on meeting him that life is not straightforward for him. 'He is a gift from Allah,' we were frequently told. Shopping is not simple in Egypt, even for the rest of us, and Tom's money problems made bartering nearly impossible. You expect to finish up paying about a quarter of the original price quoted. Unfortunately this did not work with Tom. While I was trying to walk coolly away saying, 'Far too expensive,' Tom was jumping up and down and probably offering to pay more! Luckily, by staying in the one town for the week, the locals came to know him and soon realised that he couldn't grasp the game of bartering. After paying far too much at the start of the week, we finished up with him being given a number of presents.

Luxor is full of ancient monuments to visit. Without Tom we might have visited more but Tom had his limit so, after camel riding, we opted for a day travelling to a Nubian village on donkeys. Hadji, the donkey man, took us for mint tea at his mother-in-law's home in the village and afterwards invited us to lunch at his own home. Buffalo cheese, omelette and salad eaten from communal dishes, while kneeling at the table in a home with no running water or electricity and with a bread oven outside and just twenty yards from the Nile — a wonderful way for Tom to learn about geography, history, religion and the other peoples of the world. He insisted on giving Hadji his Walkman as a thank you present and we returned from the holiday valuing our 'gift from Allah' even more.

One more incident on a holiday needs mentioning here as it marked another milestone in Tom's maturity. Shortly after the trip to Egypt, Tom and I went to Naples to see Beatrice who was living out there for a while. At Naples airport on Easter Day 1996, I experienced one of those moments when you long for the floor to open up and suck you in, or for a fairy godmother to wave a wand and remove you from the scene. Embarrassment in its worst form.

Tom had a new and complex Walkman after giving his old one to Hadji in Luxor. It was the type of machine that allows you to listen to both sides of the tape without turning it over. It was too elaborate for him to manage. He was listening to a story, using his earphones, while we waited to be called to the boarding gate. He stopped it to speak to me and then pressed the wrong start knob and the tape continued but on the reverse side. He tried another knob but still couldn't get back to where he had been. He became more and more frustrated, pressed every button, turned the tape over, jumped up, sat down, stamped his foot, shouted. Heads turned in our direction. Why was this large lad behaving like a toddler in a tantrum? This was the moment when I wanted to disappear.

I took the tape machine away to try to sort it out but I have never used a Walkman and couldn't resolve the problem anyway as I didn't know which bit of the story he had been listening to, so I was completely helpless to assist.

A feeling of helplessness leads me to anger but I knew that was the last emotion needed on my part now. If I showed my frustration with his behaviour, he would be worse still. I had to stay calm and soothing. This probably irritated him even more!

Then suddenly, almost as quickly as the scene had arisen, it ended. He sat down and turned to me. 'Mum,' he said sheepishly, 'it's Easter Sunday — chocolate.' It then dawned on me too that we had started the day in Naples having an Easter breakfast with Beatrice and her boyfriend. We knew Tom was allergic to chocolate, so had kept the eggs to a minimum, but it is hard to have none, especially as Bea loves chocolate and we were leaving her that day. Chocolate on an empty stomach is like dynamite to Tom and for years, until we realised this, Easter Sunday was a particularly stressful day.

I no longer cared that half the airport crowd was still gazing at us. I was just so pleased that Tom had seen for himself his reaction to chocolate so that, hopefully, in future it would not be the cruel mother denying him the taste he loves, but Tom reminding us not to give him Easter eggs. The following year, as Easter loomed, he asked for a video instead of an egg.

Tom's next trip is now planned. When he leaves his course in Brighton he is keen to have a Gap year. He saw his sister leave school and, before going to university, work in London for six months to pay for the next six months of teaching in China. He has also listened to his cousins talk about their experiences in Nepal and Vietnam. He has been saving his money ready but we wondered where he could go and how his dream could be fulfilled. You cannot take your parents on such a venture. It would lose much of its purpose.

Our town has a friendship link with Kisumu in Kenya and over the years we have had a few Kenyans to visit us. Last year Jane and Beldina, two Kenyan teachers, came to stay for a fortnight and were keen on a trip to Brighton to see Tom. When they heard about his desire to travel, they invited him to stay. Both have sons of his age. At Easter I visited them to see for myself what the situation will be for Tom and now his flight is booked. I feel anxious as I write and Tom recognises that, come the time to travel and the panic feelings set in for him, he may have difficulty getting himself dressed to go. However our agreement with him is that we will get him to the airport however he is feeling on the day. He wants this trip and doesn't want it ruined by a panic attack. British Airways assisted travel service will take over from there. Jane and Beldina have promised to meet him and I know we can rely on them. I think he realises it is a Gap month rather than a year. However long it is, it will be a big adventure for him which, if successful, will boost his self-esteem and help him grow in confidence.

Part Two

Ten

Patterns

The process of writing Tom's story so far has been a power-ful, healing and revealing experience for me. I have an image of a large map spread out on the ground, with a road marked on it that represents our journey together as a family. The road is wide enough for the four of us to walk along and I can see how sometimes we have been diverted down a seem-ingly dead-end track and have had to turn round and come back. In fact these detours have often helped to enrich our lives even though we could not see it at the time. Beatrice has taken her own path more and more frequently as she has grown older, returning every now and again to join in with us. Tom, on the other hand, has so far only taken tentative or coerced (as in the case of boarding school) trips away from his parents. Mostly he still likes to be on the same road as us, preferably walking hand in hand, but this, we hope, is beginning to change. Along the road I can see milestones representing events and people in our lives. It is all so much clearer to me now.

Initially, as I looked back over the years of his childhood, I was surprised at how much pain I continued to carry around, well hidden in my unconscious. When I wrote about the support from my mother, especially in having Tom to stay each month, I found myself in tears. The rea-son for them is still unclear. It is probably the fact that she noticed we needed help. I have also discovered pockets of embedded anger stemming from years ago, such as my feel-ings over Tom's exclusion from the Findhorn playgroup. Most of all, the writing has made me more conscious of the process that we as a family have gone through and I have also taken the opportunity to listen to and read the stories of other parents. By doing this I have come to understand much more clearly the role of carers and what they experience. Seeing the process has given me a chance to deal with and release still-buried hurt and anger, so freeing me to move on in life, and providing an opportunity to thank those who have helped. Listening to others, I have been able to see the themes and patterns that run through all the stories, as often the same comments and descriptions occur in each person's experience. Each theme brings with it its own set of lessons and opportunities to grow and learn. These themes include expectations, tension and exhaustion, isolation and searching.

Expectations

Tom's life continues to unfold and develop. He is a fine young man now, nineteen years old, and often wondering what he will be doing in the future. Will he get a job? Will he get married and have children? We have all, by now, learnt lessons in his lifetime. An important one has been not to look too far ahead into the future. When he was born, I already had his life planned, at least for as long as I would have influence over it. I expected him to be part of the group of parents and children who were around us in the Findhorn Foundation. I hoped he would become good friends with my best friend's son, who was three weeks younger, and together we would while away the childhood hours, Tom and Michael playing while Liza and I chatted. I did realise that children chose their own friends but at least there was a good choice around him and I liked most of the mothers. I imagined us going on family holidays, sharing accommodation with another family with similar-aged children — perhaps a French farmhouse, where the children would swim and play tennis while the parents sat around the pool, eating olives and drinking the local wine. I can still see it in my mind, despite the fact that it never happened!

In this idyllic childhood, Tom would join clubs and learn sports. I am very keen on the latter and looked forward to

Tom's company at cricket matches, perhaps even with him playing. Most of the men in my family have gone to Winchester for their schooling and it was my dream that he would go there too, if we could possibly afford it. It was money I thought might spoil the dream, not ability. From school it would be university and then a 'good' job.

What a heavy burden to put on any child. My plans for Beatrice have moved and shifted over the years but she has more than fulfilled my dreams, so I had no reason to expect things would be different with Tom. It may sound naive. We all know of children who have problems to a degree but we protect ourselves from the danger by believing it is not going to happen to us. It was this very dream of Tom's future that made it so hard to recognise the truth in the situation. Each time he surprised us with a poem or an intelligent remark, I clung to this as proof that all would be well and he would grow out of his difficulties. It took to the age of thirteen before the message got through to me that Tom had fundamental problems in understanding and dealing with life. The paediatrician who spelt out to us that Tom was 'mentally retarded' and the headmistress who described him as 'an eccentric' brought home the truth. I heard them and my expectations fell away. I stopped planning further than the next year into the future. I learnt to say, 'I don't know,' when asked the frequent question by friends about what Tom would do in the future and how he would manage.

It must have been a great relief for Tom when I at last released my expectations. I was able to start seeing him for who he was and not who I wanted him to be. I read an article recently by a parent of a child with learning difficulties. When writing about the early years of her daughter's childhood she says, 'Would we have tried so hard to make her walk if we had known she had severe learning difficulties? Would I have been more patient with her slow eating if I had known this was common in babies like her? I wonder whether I would have enjoyed her more if I had expected less.' Her article moved me as I identified with the struggles she and her family went through — struggles which had much in common with our own experience.

I am certain that parents of more able children can equally relate to the tensions created by the effect of their expectations on their children. The father who hopes his son will fulfil his own dreams of being an international footballer or the mother whose daughter, while capable of joining in with normal schooling, is not as academically inclined as the rest of the family. Both children could be pushed to breaking point before the expectations of their parents are lifted, or they may in fact achieve more because of the parental pressure than they would have done. There is a very fine line between the benefits and disadvantages of such pressure. Certainly I believe Tom suffered as a result of my unrealistic hopes for him but he will also achieve more because we have refused to drop them completely.

Hopes and expectations can be a trap that even Tom falls into. Recently he said, 'If my son's brainy, I'd like to send him to a top school and university and then I'll feel he has fulfilled things for me.' This is an echo of my early expectations which he has clearly picked up and understood. I hope that he, like me, will learn to release them, as we both come to recognise his true value as he is.

The current plan is for Tom to live at home and attend the local Technical College, which has a department for youngsters with special needs. We hope to find him other educational courses for the next two or three years which will give him time to continue to mature and develop and further prepare him for the rest of his journey through life. I cannot answer his questions about his future. In some ways he has done so much better than our adjusted expectations and in other ways he continues to fall increasingly behind his peer group as his limitations, such as lack of number, inhibit his ability to step forward into the world on his own. What I can see now is that he takes with him some real strengths of character which will help him to make the most of each situation with which he is faced.

Isolation

There are so many families in the world in a similar situation to ourselves and yet we, and others I have talked to, have a pervading sense of isolation. In conversation with a friend who has a terminally ill and brain-damaged husband I asked if she belonged to a support group for carers. 'Oh no,' she said, 'I don't think there are other people in my situation.' From outside I could see that this was highly unlikely to be the case. Carers of stroke victims or spouses with Alzheimer's must experience many of the same problems even if the illness in question is different. Although my friend was not looking after a disabled child, her feeling of isolation was the same as we had experienced. Surely with so many children like Tom around, we should have had a sense of unity and support. It appears that a number of factors have led to this perceived isolation.

First, it seems that historically in Britain disabled children have been an embarrassment and source of shame to their families and have been hidden away. When I was a child, I hardly ever saw our neighbour's daughter, despite the fact that she was only a few years older than I was and I went to school and played with her brothers. I think she disappeared into an institution as soon as she reached puberty and started to behave 'inappropriately' towards the boys around. I don't really know, as she was never talked about in front of me. Even nowadays it can take a while after making new friends to discover they have a disabled child. A friend put this down to the glazed look that comes into people's eyes when she mentions her daughter. It is probably not lack of interest on their part but rather confusion as they don't know what to say.

The issue of shame and parental blame should be long gone but I hear echoes of it as, after talking about Tom, I catch myself dropping into the conversation that Beatrice is at Oxford University, as if to prove that as parents we are capable of producing a bright child. Shame and isolation also come from the attitude of society to disablement which is nearly always viewed as a negative situation. Even the word 'disabled' means 'not being able'. Often the first people involved are doctors and the rest of the medical world, who define children by what they cannot do, and by what the 'illness' is and whether it can be cured. Alternatively, disabled children are seen as having suffered a disaster, although with help from the able-bodied world they may manage to achieve against the odds. When we learn to see so-called 'disabled children' as complete and perfect in themselves and that it is society which needs to adapt and recognise all they have to offer, parents will be helped to do the same. Then, it is to be hoped, they will no longer carry a sense of shame or blame which isolates them.

I have been very slow in moving in this direction but I can remember the first few times I recognised Tom's strengths as being born out of his difficulties. When he was introduced to the toy Lego as a very small child, Tom, unlike his friends, was unable to follow the diagrams from the back of the box and create the expected model. His friends learnt one set of skills from the toy. He, however, would join two or three pieces together and in his head it was already a car or aeroplane and he would leap up and be off round the room weaving an intricate story involving his 'model'. In the process, he may have antagonised his companions by stepping on them and their creations but his way of using the toy allowed his imagination to blossom. Today, perhaps, we can see the fruits of this when he suggests to us that he would like to write an opera based on the stories of Dr Who!

Time has definitely changed attitudes for the better but, even living in a 'spiritual community', it felt that Tom's problems were our problem, not the community's, and an embarrassment to all, because no one knew how to deal with the situation.

An added factor in the isolation was the difficulty in diagnosing Tom. I stated earlier that I often wished his 'problems' had been easier to diagnose. A Down's syndrome baby is recognisable at birth or shortly afterwards and there are active and valuable support groups. I still have not belonged to such a group relating to Tom, but presume that they create the opportunity to express the pain caused by the situation in which the parents find themselves and to realise that such feelings are normal. They would also help parents to understand the processes they go through as they learn to adapt to and cope with their role as carers. I realise now, too, that there must be textbooks on the subject that you would find out about in such support groups.

I was recently contacted by a new organisation called WATCHWORD (What About These Children Without Recognised Diagnosis). Apparently about forty per cent of children with learning difficulties are never diagnosed with a named condition and the organisation plans to link together parents who are in a similar predicament. With no clear diagnosis, the parents don't have the same opportunity to start mourning the loss of their dreams and expectations, a very important part of the process for carers. It was not until Tom was twelve or thirteen that we were able to go through the necessary mourning. This entails sadness and anger but also allows you to move on and face the new situation.

I was recently shown a diagram (see overleaf) depicting the usual pattern of behaviour that people go through when faced with loss. In our situation we were dealing with our loss of hopes and expectations around our son's future, including his lifestyle, status and dignity.

I remember vividly the shock I felt as I heard the strange, clear voice in my head while lying in bed in hospital in Inverness. Then the denial stage set in and lasted, in varying degrees, until Tom was nearly thirteen. What amused and pleased me most when shown this diagram was to see that in writing this book I have focused on looking at the gains. While recognising that, when setbacks occur, it is possible to reverse at times into the depressed and angry stages, I can see that quite unconsciously we have worked our way through the process of mourning and have, most of the time, reached the other side.

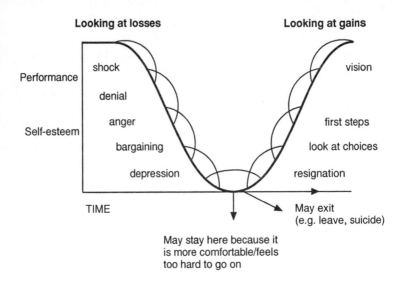

The mourning process and especially the period of denial help to reinforce the isolation. Tom didn't fit in with many able-bodied groups of children but we were still trying not to see him as disabled. Even when we did look for friends among the latter group it was hard because all the children vary in their abilities and frequently don't play well together. Rather than being linked by their disabilities we discovered they were separated by them, and by their abilities. One boy, Jason, whom we tried inviting home from St Vincent's Assessment Centre, could read but not walk, while Tom could walk but not read. As they had little in common they didn't find it easy to spend time in each other's company. This difficulty in finding 'similar' children made it awkward to form informal support groups with other parents.

WATCHWORD sends out a newsletter and one item was a description of a mother's experience which concluded with, 'It's good to know there are more children like John and it's good for us to know that we are not on our own' — an example of another mother who has felt the isolation.

I have described how, over the years, we attempted to find children and families with whom to do things, both chil-

dren like Jason who were disabled and able-bodied ones.
Each time a family decided, consciously or unconsciously,
not to play with Tom, for them it was just one child they were
excluding from their circle of friends. For us and Tom, over
the years, it was everybody with children. It became much
easier not to make the attempt so that none of us had to experience the inevitable rejection Even the one or two families
with youngsters who said they liked Tom and were happy
to have him round had such busy lives with their own friends
that they forgot to include him.

In looking with Nick at the sense of isolation and the let-
down that we have felt over the years around support and
help from our friends and families, we realised that it is, in
fact, a sense of our own failure to deal with the situation that
we have projected out onto others. In reality, we have many
friends who have been there for us, either directly with Tom
or in supporting us as parents, giving us holidays, counselling sessions and general moral support. It is not other
people's responsibility to help us. We are Tom's parents. We
have made the contract with him to bring him up and love
and value him.

Someone said to me recently about Tom leaving their
school, 'You'd always miss Tom. He makes the world a better place.' Have I yet reached the point where I can see this?
For me, I know that Nick and Beatrice make my world a better place. I feel joy each time I see them. Looking at Tom, I
do feel joy but it is still tempered. I am beginning to get there.
I have moved miles since the days of desperation in his childhood, but I am still working at truly valuing him. I continue,
sometimes, to find myself overwhelmed by his company.
Part of me disappears beneath his needs. That is true in all
my relationships but much more so in relationship to Tom.

I am changing but I still manage quite often to feel a failure around him. When he is home for the holidays and half-
term, I feel I fail him most days. Much of his time is spent
watching television. He needs others to motivate him and I
cannot do that all the time. Nick has usually amused him by

taking him for long walks on their own or trawling through charity shops for interesting pieces of clothing. I arrange trips to the gym, dog-walking with my friends, the cinema, tea at Granny's, but they are all time-filling activities, while I wait for Tom to take charge of his life. If someone else asks Tom out for the day, my sense of failure lifts while he is out.

I feel a responsibility to 'amuse him' which I do not experience with Beatrice or Nick. I may have felt it with Beatrice when she was very small but she soon took over that responsibility for herself, suggesting places to go or things to do or arranging them on her own. At present, as I become conscious of my feelings, perhaps I begin to see a change in the situation with Tom. If I stopped feeling responsible for his entertainment and just left him to the television, hopefully he would start to motivate himself. I will certainly have to try it out. However, his problem is not just breaking free of the emotional dependence on us, his parents, but all the practical issues of doing things on his own; the problems with time, money, transport and shyness with others that keep him trapped in his dependence.

Given that I feel we all chose to be together as a family and that we are teachers to each other, Tom needs to learn to break free of our control — not easy as the pattern is well entrenched. For Nick, being with Tom makes him very aware of his sense of not having enough: not enough time or energy or ability to cope. These are attitudes that he is now working to change.

The sense of isolation has also strengthened our family unit. We have learnt how to have a happy holiday together, and have discovered the pleasure of house-sitting for others. As a family we have been thrown together and have learnt to enjoy it. In fact, likening family life to a classroom does not mean all the lessons are uncomfortable. We have certainly had many good laughs, especially once we realised that Tom was intending to be funny.

Beatrice comments, 'One of the qualities I most enjoy in Tom is his sense of humour. He has provided our family with much merriment as he still frequently appears in the guise of vicars, colonels or kilted Highlanders, with even the occasional suspender belt thrown in for good measure! He then creates a whole persona with accents and mannerisms which he achieves very accurately — he is a true 'actor'. Half the town must have heard Tom booming Alec Guinness's intriguing line in *Kind Hearts and Coronets*, "Do you speak Matabele?" at everyone he meets. Admittedly, as a bashful teenager I would wince when Tom would attempt to sally forth into town in his wacky wardrobe and I would refuse to go with him unless he changed into something a little more subdued.'

She continues, 'I also love the way Tom experiences life so fully. Obviously it has its ups and downs, but it means he will really enjoy something wholeheartedly. Unfortunately, when we were younger, Tom would always laugh so much that he would wet himself. So when, for example, he would roll around with laughter at the mouldy apples on the lawn, which for some reason he found hysterically funny, we would be desperately trying to manoeuvre him to the nearest loo. Poor Mum must have been inundated with washing as Tom used to do a lot of laughing!'

Beatrice, four years older than Tom, accepted her role as an additional parent and from an early age helped in taking responsibility for him. She, too, even attempted to give him reading lessons. Today, when she is around, she will take him swimming or have him to stay at her shared university flat, taking him to the pub with her friends, and she has a deep love for and loyalty to him. As a child, she didn't find it easy. She would seldom invite school friends home. In her teens her closest friends were those who had similar difficult situations at home with their fathers or brothers. They understood each other, often even without discussing the pressures they were under. Living with Tom as a brother may well have strengthened Beatrice's character and has certainly given her knowledge and insights around disability which many other youngsters might not have learnt.

I hope that if I were to live through Tom's childhood again, with the knowledge and experience I have gained, I would now have some idea of how to work with others, both individuals and families, to help them embrace Tom into their lives. When looking for friends for Tom, once I had accepted that he had problems, I was viewing disablement as needing charity. (Poor Tom, he needs help. It is up to the able-bodied to be kind and solve the situation.) I hoped others would satisfy his need for playmates and give us a break. When Tom was rejected and ejected from a social situation we were hurt and we dealt with the pain by withdrawing into ourselves as a family.

If I now view the same scenario using the social model of disability (disabled people are seen, like everyone else, as having wants, needs and aspirations; they don't need pity or a cure and aspects of their disability can be seen as positive assets; society needs to adapt itself to make use of these assets), immediately I can see that by rejecting Tom the other family is missing an opportunity for pleasure and growth. I would today, I hope, have the courage to ask why Tom is being turned away and use my skills in negotiating to discover how all involved could be helped to deal with the situation more positively. When Tom was young I couldn't see what he was able to give to the other family, such as his fun, his openness, his original thinking. I could only see the difficulties he caused for them.

Recently my sister mentioned that her daughter had thought about including Tom at her party but had decided not to do so. There were good reasons for this decision. They are not close and he knows none of her friends. On this occasion, I was able to acknowledge this and to say, 'It's the right decision but it's a pity, as he's looking forward to being invited to parties.' Later, my sister rang again. She and her daughter had talked it over and suggested that they invite him to visit on another weekend and that he would go to the pub with his cousin and one or two of her friends. Instead of feeling hurt by Tom's exclusion, I had been able to express his need and the other family had adapted their plans to fit him in. Now his cousin has a chance to discover what fun he can be!

Using this social model of defining disability is very empowering to both the disabled person and their carers. When the able-bodied in society take the time to adjust and get to know a person like Tom, the benefits are reciprocal. Tom gives as much as he receives. Now that I understand this, I can look back to the friend in my Girl Guide troop, whose legs were paralysed by polio. We had to adapt our behaviour to allow her to join in with us and then found that she was definitely an asset to our swimming team as, even without using her legs, she could swim faster than most of us. She came with us on a small camp run by my sisters. We had to learn to assist her with her leg irons and crutches and to adapt the holiday to include her. She, in return, became a good friend.

Tension and exhaustion

Tension and exhaustion go hand in hand and are a feature of all the stories I have heard and read. All mothers have experienced tension and exhaustion while their children were toddlers. What are they going to climb on next? Will they escape my hand near a main road? Have they learnt to open the front door yet? In the case of most children this is an intense phase which passes relatively quickly. With children like Tom it can continue for years.

When Tom was young, he took on the role of defender of the vulnerable. He hated to see a parent telling off their child and would rush in with his comments — behaviour which was never popular with the fraught parent, who was quite likely to turn on Tom himself. We needed to be on the look-out for any such scenario and to divert Tom swiftly in another direction.

And it was not just the young he would defend. On one occasion Nick was with him in a shop. As they approached the till, the assistant arrived and slid into her seat to take their money. Almost immediately, the manager came up and started telling her off for being late. The next thing Nick heard was, 'Don't you talk to her like that. She can be late if she wants to be. You are a very rude woman!' It was Tom, and there was a ghastly hush while everyone looked at him. Then luckily they all started to laugh, including the manager, and the tension of the moment was released. When they moved to the next counter, Tom was greeted with great friendliness by the assistants with, 'You're the little boy who ticked off our manager' — thus setting him up for the next time he saw an injustice.

Another example of a tension-creating incident was that experienced by Nick when he was waiting with Tom at a bus station to collect somebody one day. A man was sitting in his car, eating sweets and dropping the wrappers out of his window. Tom walked over, picked them up and posted them back through the window saying, 'Don't drop litter!' Nick had to hurry him away before the man could get out of his car and punch him. The difficulty with these last two incidents was that Tom was actually in the right but was not behaving in a socially acceptable way. Our society believes that small children should not tell off adults, particularly strangers. Tension caused by being constantly on one's guard against the next 'incident' leads to an ongoing feeling of exhaustion. One major role that parents are supposed to fulfil is to socialise their children. With a child like Tom, who didn't fit the 'normal' mode (if such a thing exists) and found it hard to grasp the rules of society, one never knew what would happen next and we frequently felt we were failures despite all our best efforts and constant nagging.

The subject of exhaustion leads on to the need for respite care and the lack of funding of Social Services. This, however, is a political issue and not appropriate for this story, especially as we managed, with the support of my mother, to avoid asking for help. The only problem is that it would probably have improved our parenting if we had been given more breaks in the early days but it is very hard to ask and for a long time Social Services were not aware of us at all. We felt we should be able to manage and to ask would have been a sign of our failure. This was exacerbated by the fact that we are both qualified social workers so that even though Tom, at twelve, became an 'open case' at Social Services, they were so short of staff and finance that they were able to presume we could manage without their help. At the suggestion of another mother, we did pay a vast amount for Tom, at the age of about six, to go away for a week to a lady who ran respite holidays. She was a kind person and the time was packed with interesting activities but he hated going and we felt very guilty about sending him and didn't try it again.

We did summon up the courage to ask one close person to have Tom to stay but the refusal, when it came, was so painful that we resisted asking others. Eventually the respite came in the form of boarding school. Now, as this has come to an end, we realise that we have learnt to recognise our own limitations and needs better and to see that seeking help is not a sign of failure. We have already contacted the charity Mencap and again the local Social Services to give us all, including Tom, help in dealing with the next stage of his life.

Hearing another mother's story of respite care was also an opportunity to hear about her growth as an individual and her opening as a human being. Once a month her son stays with another family for the weekend. This support family comes from a background totally dissimilar to hers. They are the sort of family she would have had little contact with under normal circumstances and would have dismissed due to class differences and prejudice. It took her time to learn to trust them with her son and to believe that they could care for him as well as she did. By now she has total trust in and respect for this family. She can see that they love her son as their own and he enjoys staying with them. The experience has helped her to look at some of her prejudices and to move through them.

Searching

A constant and ongoing search seems to be part of the process that the parents to whom I have spoken have gone through. I expect the search is different if the diagnosis comes earlier. In that case the search is probably for the best treatments, schools and support for that particular problem. In our case it was a search for a diagnosis first and foremost with, we hoped, a cure attached to it.

For those I have spoken to, the searching appears to have a cyclical feature to it. We certainly went through periods of intense activity following some particular thread in our quest for a solution or a school. Then, exhausted, we would rest and recuperate and wait to summon up the energy to start again when the next lead came along. The cycles also swung between orthodox medicine and alternative therapies and between government schools and psychologists and the private sector.

If we had understood Tom's problems earlier, we might have had more help from the medical and educational authorities in focusing our enquiries in a relevant direction. Part of the time is wasted in finding out about all the available schools and treatments, especially as each group seems to know very little about any other. For example, our Local Education Authority, despite their own limited variety of establishments, gave us no information on private schools until they were forced to when we won our Appeal. It would be extremely helpful if someone created a comprehensive directory to save each family from having to rediscover all that is out there to be found.

Looking for a school without a clear diagnosis confuses the issue and uses up more time. Our long days out on visits and our raised hopes and expectations followed by disappointment seemed a waste of energy when they happened. In reality the process widened our knowledge and understanding of the whole subject of disablement and we learnt about many different types of treatment and approaches to education and saw some really excellent and varied schools.

We visited both government schools and private ones and saw the contrast between our local school for children with Moderate Learning Difficulties, with few facilities, and the dyslexia departments of some of the most expensive private schools in the country. We looked at Steiner Schools and learnt about their philosophies and saw units where work is done with youngsters with cerebral palsy, inspired by the Peto Institute in Hungary. We also tried amazing new computer technology used in schools for the physically disabled. It is likely that we would have seen and done none of this if we hadn't been searching for the right place for Tom. We tried orthodox medicine, with scans and EEGs, and alternative medicine, with exercises, hair analysis and the Alexander Technique. We threw the net wide enough to include spiritual healing, each type with its own set of beliefs to absorb. Undoubtedly we learnt and gained something from every contact we made.

For the past three years we have hardly searched at all. Tom has been happy at St John's School. We have had confidence in the teaching and it has been a relief to relax and give up looking for a while. But the searching hasn't ended. With Tom's return to live at home, it becomes easier to try out new suggestions. Recently we have heard of various original and unusual ways to assist youngsters with learning difficulties. These include such ideas as swimming with dolphins off the west coast of Ireland and Tomatis sound therapy. Both appear to stimulate the brain through sound and can, supposedly, have startling effects. Both would also mean more travel and money and further raised expectations, with the potential for more disappointment in their wake.

Recently we were given an article about children with 'William's syndrome', a genetic learning disability caused by a small, missing chunk of DNA on chromosome 7. The description of the children affected has a number of similarities to Tom, including very good use of language, sociability (often beyond the acceptable) and problems with number, writing, coordination and spatial awareness. It would seem worth exploring but I immediately feel hesitant. First, we would have to approach the medical profession with yet another possible diagnosis which they may have missed. I would need to feel very confident to summon up the courage to do this. More importantly, perhaps, I realise that I am not sure now that I want a genetic diagnosis. Up until Tom was thirteen I would have been delighted to know what was wrong. But times have changed and so has Tom. My worry now would be that I would have to accept Tom's limitations as immutable if they are caused by chromosomes. What would we gain by knowing that he can never change? Maybe I have not let go of my expectations and hopes as well as I had thought I had, and perhaps that is a good thing.

Co-Dependency

I learnt about the concept of co-dependency as a probation officer, initially in relation to alcoholics and other addicts. It took a long time for me to realise that co-dependency could apply to the carers and family of a disabled child.

One day recently, Tom and I walked into town. First we stopped at a shop to buy a computer game for Tom. I did the talking and the assistant found the game for us. Tom was planning to pay for it and I told him the price and asked him to produce the cash from his purse for the transaction. I went through a whole performance of trying to help him calculate the notes necessary. As we left the shop, I was already questioning my motives for the scene we had just enacted. Was I trying to help him manage his money and learn how many and which notes to produce? Was I helping to build his confidence at shopping? Or did I have another motive?

We walked further into town. Tom was due to catch a bus to visit his grandmother in a neighbouring village. He has travelled by bus in Brighton with other children or teachers from his college but this was a first for him at home. We had discovered a few days earlier how much the fare would be and where and when the bus left and Tom had practised asking for his ticket. My mother had promised she would not meet him at the bus stop, as he only had one road to cross, at traffic lights, and had assured us that he knew the way to her house. (In fact she was so anxious that she circumvented the promise by asking a friend, who was a stranger to Tom, to go and watch him off the bus!)

The bus arrived and I stepped back and let Tom climb aboard. I too felt so anxious about letting him go alone that I didn't move far enough away. Despite his rehearsal and despite having the exact change in his hand, he turned to me instead of the driver. On cue I moved forward and told him to ask for the ticket. Immediately everyone was aware of his problems. The driver said, 'Don't worry, I'll tell him when to get off,' and I watched him sit down, and left.

As I walked away, I again thought about my behaviour. If I had stood further away, Tom would have bought his ticket and sat down just like all the other passengers. By hovering close by, I undermined his uncertain self-assurance. He turned to me for help. From this, in my head, I gained the unspoken praise of the driver and nearby passengers. 'What a good mother, helping her disabled son. What hard work it must be for her.' The performance in the shop could well have given me the same reward: acknowledgement of the time and effort it takes to bring up a disabled child. The good resolution to this story was told to me by my mother. When Tom reached her house and knocked on her door, she opened it to find him beaming from ear to ear, saying, 'I did it. I did it.'

These incidents are not told in order to put myself down but because they were the dawning of awareness in recognising my co-dependence on Tom's problems. When one member of the family has problems, the rest must adapt to cope with the situation. Tom's difficulties have meant that Nick, Beatrice and I have all had to change our lives to help him and to survive the pressure created by the situation.

Nick and I have put, and continue to put, extra hours into our role as parents and have become used to this role and thus, to a certain extent, dependent on Tom's problems. If Tom wants to change and mature, we must do so too. If Tom becomes more independent, it is a threat to my role as his carer. I have learnt to value myself as the dedicated mother of a disabled child and I would no longer have him as an excuse not to face other issues.

Another friend with a disabled son described her experience when first given monthly respite care. Her son left on Friday evening but not until half way through Saturday could she relax. At first she would feel bereft, a sense of loss both of her son and her identity. Without him she was unsure what to do or even who she was. She can see that the family use him as an excuse not to address other conflicts, or make decisions or do things. She feels most of the grief and anger felt in the family is focused around this son.

Prader-Willi syndrome is a complex genetic disorder associated with chromosome 15. Like some other syndromes, the children have a particular look. They need close care and control in their lives as, among various factors, they lack the normal message that tells them when they have eaten enough. They are constantly hungry and searching for food, even perhaps ransacking a room in hopes of finding a chocolate bar left by a brother or sister. They can easily become massively overweight, leading to severe health problems. The intensity and dedication needed to care for such a child is obvious. By the age of nineteen, one friend's daughter wanted to leave home and organised for herself to move into a supportive community a few miles away. Initially, instead of being able to welcome the new time and space in her own life, her mother found the parting very distressing and spent much time sitting and watching in her car outside the home. She told me that at the time she felt that she knew her daughter and that nobody else would cope with her problems as she had coped and nobody else could do things for her as she had done, and that her daughter would miss out. She also felt that nobody else should tell her daughter off. Only her family should be doing that. She found it very hard initially to lose her role as carer and to move on in her life.

Tom is about to live at home with us again full time and is very keen to do so. Simultaneously he is soon to embark on this great adventure, his trip to Africa. Releasing him from our dependence on him is part of the process we are currently going through. If he can travel on his own to Africa, what is our role in the future? I recently returned from my visit there and brought back with me a six-inch-high model African hut that I had been given. It was sitting on the table along with the wooden spoons and baskets I had also collected. Tom gazed at it for a while and then said, 'Mum, I'm a bit worried. I'm not sure that I'll be able to fit into a house like that to sleep.'

At first we thought he was joking but then recognised that he was serious. I realised that I had put it on the table saying, 'This is an African house.' I had omitted the word 'model'.

'But Tom, you know Jane and Beldina. They wouldn't fit in there either. They are too big.'

'Oh yes,' he says, 'they would have to shrink to this high,' holding his hand about three feet off the ground. When he was young he had often asked, 'Which is bigger, a house or grand piano?' and other such questions about size. We hadn't realised that it was still an area of difficulty for him. With confusions like that to deal with, let alone foreign money and his shyness about asking for help, it is certainly going to be a big adventure and a real test for us as his parents in releasing him.

When I went to Kenya, I bought a very cheap plane ticket. It was cheap because it couldn't be changed. I had presumed that I would be able to cope with the experience. Tom is paying for a much more expensive flight which allows for flexibility in case he decides not to go or needs to come home earlier. Is this the sensible thing to do and the act of caring parents to build in a safety net? Or is this also part of the co-dependency which, by doubting his ability to manage, will undermine his confidence in himself? Again we meet a very fine line between doing the right thing or not. This is a dilemma faced not only by fathers and mothers of disabled children; it will undoubtedly be recognised by all parents as their children grow up.

As I write, I am watching a man walking his Siamese cat down the road on a long string. I look at him often. He is tall, slim and middle-aged with shoulder-length hair and he meanders very slowly past our house two or three times a day, while the cat explores. Occasionally I say hello to him and exchange a remark or two, but I know nothing about his life or how he sees the world. He feels to me like a walk-on character in the play of my life — a play in which I cannot help but take the leading role as it is through myself that I experience the world. I assume that each person is living on their own stage set. I have occasional glimpses into other people's views of life, mostly those of my family and close friends and sometimes those of strangers who unburden themselves to me.

At the start of a child's life, mother and baby are close-ly linked and spend much of their time together. It didn't take long for Beatrice to find her own role and now, although from time to time she will share her experiences with me, there is inevitably much that I know little about. Tom has remained far closer. He has found it harder to move away. For Beatrice, it was a gradual process with a greater leap during adolescence. Tom has yet to make that jump and, as a result, we are still fully involved in all the impor-tant decisions he has to make and many of the minor ones. When he is with us, we hear exactly what is going on for him, especially his feelings. He seems to have few of the nor-mal adolescent secrets, particularly in respect of his sexual development or his general likes and dislikes. In many ways it is a real privilege to share his life and perspectives so intensely, to be actors with him on the same stage. The trick will be not to hang on to him and expect the same role when he is ready to grow away from us.

There comes a moment for parents when they no longer need to mother or father their children, except on the odd occasion. It is to be hoped that they can then become supportive friends. Beatrice, aged twenty-three, is definitely a good friend of mine and Nick's and has been for some years. Tom is aware of this and tells us he is looking forward to having a similar relationship, especially with his father, so that they can go to the pub together and chat over a pint. He even tells us that he will look after us in our old age and, as a result of an awkward incident he had on a work experience in an old people's home, says he will do a course on how to change our nappies! Then our roles will really have come full circle.

Returning to the concept of co-dependency, I can see that when Tom went to boarding school and Nick and I couldn't get out of bed at weekends, we were demonstrating an aspect of this. We had lost some of the ability to see ourselves and to motivate ourselves when not in our role as Tom's parents. Bringing this concept into our awareness is the first step in unravelling the unsatisfactory cords that tie us all together. I hope we will always be linked by the bonds of love and friendship to both our children, but the needy bonds that harness us together and stop all of us developing as mature individuals need cutting.

Eleven

Changing attitudes

Travelling through life with Tom has been a creative and learning experience for us all and in order to cope with the stresses and strains of the process we have used many 'techniques' to keep us going. Three in particular have strengthened and supported us.

Re-evaluation co-counselling

Re-evaluation co-counselling was the first. When we moved to the Findhorn Foundation in 1975 it was a place of idealism, aimed at embodying perfection. 'All is very, very well' became a catchphrase of the community. Peter Caddy, one of its co-founders, expected perfection in everything. Not surprisingly, all was not very, very well or perfect. It never can be when a very mixed group of individuals live together. Many young people came to stay and tried hard to live up to the expectation of perfection but failed. Negativity was present but not expressed and eventually, after four or five months, some members would leave and then let out the negativity they had been holding back by complaining about the community and the 'New Age'. I have described how I felt when first living there in our horrible, tiny caravan, separated from my friends and family in England.

Obviously things had to change if the community was to continue to grow and blossom. The change came through the introduction of such counselling techniques as bio-energetics, co-counselling and rebirthing. Negative emotions were recognised as existing and given a safe and appropriate place for expression. Nick and I, like many community members, became involved in re-evaluation co-counselling. We attended classes and counselled with friends and eventually I taught classes both at the Foundation and when we moved back to England. We seldom have a formal counselling session now but the theory and techniques have become a part of our lives and continue to support us in periods of stress. After its introduction to the community, people found that they were able to stay there longer as members and to settle down to family life.

Because of its importance to us over the next few years in giving us a tool with which to express and understand our feelings, which were so often overwhelming, I want to take a moment to explain more about it. Re-evaluation co-counselling was started by Harvey Jackins in the USA and is based on the belief that all babies are born loving and open human beings but that, as we go through life, we experience painful situations which gradually close us down. If when a child is hurt or frightened or angry it is allowed to express those feelings by crying, shaking or releasing the anger, the pain is healed and the child is able to evaluate the experience and learn from it. If, on the other hand, as often happens, the parent tries to stop the tears with an ice cream or a smack, the healing is not completed, nor are the lessons learnt. The crying is not the pain itself, it is way the body heals the pain. Distracting the child may make life more comfortable for the parent, but it does not heal the pain. Next time something similar happens, the emotions expressed will include the earlier hurt that has not yet been healed. If we have frequently repeated and similar painful experiences, we develop ways of coping which can eventually stick with us as rigid patterns of behaviour, no longer needed in adult life but difficult to break.

On the whole Tom has not been easy to distract or shut up when he is upset, even if we wanted to. When he discovered he had lost his Tyrolean hats on our return from Austria, everybody at the airport was aware of this fact and it was very embarrassing for us. The plus side, however, to this way of dealing with upsetting situations is that when he has finished crying and shouting it is over for him. He realised that he needed to look after his luggage better and he let go of the hats. I would have kept quiet at the time and probably for ever harboured a lurking regret about losing the hats.

In co-counselling classes people are taught to counsel with each other, dividing the time available and exchanging roles of listener and client. Clients work at their own pace and the counsellor's role is mostly that of a listener and supporter. The counsellor learns useful skills in active listening while the client is taught to express his or her emotions, often after years of blocking them. Most importantly, unlike Tom, people learn how to express their emotions when it is appropriate to do so, when they have a listener who has agreed to listen, and to stop when their share of the time is finished. For someone like myself, who has always found it far too easy to cry, learning some degree of control over when and where it is appropriate to do so has been of great use. Towards the end of one's turn as client and after releasing some of the pent-up emotions comes the time for re-evaluation, often experienced as an 'Ah, yes' sensation of recognising, on an intellectual level, what has created the problem.

I had used this technique to help me adjust to living in the community and to being a mother to Beatrice. All mothers have to alter their lives, attitudes and behaviour when they have their first child and with this method I had a tool to assist me, especially when Tom came along. It was a tool that suited me and I am well aware that each person needs to find a support system to suit them. I do, however, believe that some organised and formal support for carers is necessary. It could be a support group or an individual counsellor. Kind friends will listen in an emergency but can be overwhelmed or bored on a regular basis. With co-counselling I had a legitimate space in which to express and understand the hurt and frustration I often felt. Feelings that not only stemmed from my relationship with Tom but with the doctors, education authorities, playgroup leaders and all the people who rejected him in some way.

At the end of co-counselling sessions one is encouraged to think of 'positive directions' to take out into daily life. For example, if I had been working on my feelings about my ability to be a good mother, I would agree to look out for moments during the day when I could see that I am a good mother, to counteract the persistent and undermining voice in my head which told me I was a hopeless failure in this area. These 'positive directions' led us on to working with both 'affirmations' and 'self-esteem'.

Affirmations

I believe that as human beings we have the ability to create our lives. We are not just victims of chance, tossed around by the winds of Fate. We are, to a great extent, in charge of our lives. This is not necessarily a comfortable philosophy, especially when we don't like our situations. It is much easier to blame others or bad luck for the things that go wrong. Sometimes we create well and often we do it badly. This creation takes place through thought and speech. What we think will happen often happens. We constantly send messages to ourselves which, when repeated frequently, become the truth for us.

'I never win raffles,' people say as they buy their tickets.
'I'll never find a decent job.'
'I'm no good as a mother.'
'I can't cook.'
'My memory is hopeless.'

The list could go on and on. Each time we think or make a statement we reinforce the situation. My contact with Christian Science had taught me the phrase 'Stand porter at the door of thought' — again expressing the belief that we can change things by controlling the way we think. Nick and I have found in our lives that if we want to alter our circumstances we need to change the thoughts in our heads. It isn't easy. We have had years of practice at running ourselves down.

In order to break the patterns dictating our lives, Nick and I and our friend Fiona meet together, sometimes weekly and sometimes far less frequently, to write our 'affirmations'. These are statements of how we would like our lives to be, but written in the present tense as if they had already happened. They can cover any aspect of life including the physical condition of the house, our finances, emotions and relationships. At the point of writing the affirmation one is usually thinking, feeling or experiencing the opposite. I have kept many of my old lists and I am continually surprised by what our situation used to be and the changes that have happened. When we first left the community and started our book business, our income was small and this is reflected in the sort of affirmations we wrote.

'We have a new and beautiful kitchen.'

'We have a lovely new sitting-room carpet.'

'The roof of the house is completely renovated.'

Having written down the affirmation, it can then be released to happen. It is not necessary to worry about how it will take place. It may be, as with the kitchen and carpet, that we decided we had the necessary spare cash to do the work or buy the item. With the roof it was a different story. A new roof for a large Victorian house should have cost a fortune. In fact, shortly after that statement was written, a hurricane conveniently blasted its way through the town, following a very clear route which included our road. It made large holes in our old roof, and took our next-door neighbours' chimney and the windows out of the house opposite. The insurance companies could track its path on a map and made no quibble about paying and we finished up with a completely free new roof.

As I look through the lists, I find statements written when I was in the depth of despair over my relationship with Tom and finding it hard to value and appreciate him. These include: 'Tommy is a real pleasure to have as a son. I can feel my love for him and receive it from him. I enjoy his company and look forward to spending time with him.' I remember re-reading this affirmation a few months later and being amazed that it had started to feel true.

Later I wrote: 'Tommy's education is ideally taken care of for the next few years and organised and paid for and we are all delighted with it.' This latter one was written in February 1994, when we were struggling to pay his school fees and were still waiting to hear the result of our appeal to the Secretary of State for Education. By March or April we had heard that we had won and by May had found his school in Brighton, with the blessing of our local education authority. In order to aid the process we had visualised Tom at the bottom of a moving staircase. At the top was somebody standing and saying, 'Welcome, Tom. This is the right place for you.' We even drew a little picture to help the visualisation. The purpose of the escalator was so that we released the process. Our job was to visualise Tom standing on it and moving upwards and at the top to see the end situation but it was not up to us to worry about how it came about. The staircase would take him there. It did and during the last three years we have felt he has been in the right place.

Self-esteem

Ideally all affirmations would be right for our lives and would be fulfilled instantly. In reality this doesn't happen, although enough have come about to keep us believing in the process. The major undermining factor with affirmations is poor self-esteem or lack of self-worth. If there is a little voice constantly repeating, 'I don't deserve a nice house.' 'I'm not a good mother.' 'I'm not worth the effort.' etc, etc, we will continue to sabotage our plans for a delightful and fulfilling future.

I learnt as a probation officer that people could only change their lives and behaviour if they believed that they were worth saving. I spent much of my time with criminals trying to help improve their sense of self-esteem by, for example, listing the things about themselves that they liked. They would mostly start by saying, 'There's nothing,' but those who could eventually begin to value themselves were able to make some changes in their destructive behaviour. You are less likely to fill yourself with drugs and alcohol or get yourself back into prison if you like yourself. You realise that you deserve better.

Some people's self-esteem is lower than that of others, probably relating to the experiences they endured as a child, but nearly everyone I know undermines their lives to some extent through their poor self-image or because there are aspects of their character that they don't like. School is a particular period of challenge as far as self-esteem is concerned. Children are asked to do such a variety of things and to learn so many different skills, some of which are very difficult for them, and they have the ongoing comparison of their achievements against those of their classmates. As they get older, they can opt out of the ones that they don't like or cannot do and can build on their strengths which simultaneously will increase their self-esteem.

For a child like Tom, who has made little progress in reading, writing or number over the years and hasn't been able to compensate with sporting or artistic success, it must have been extremely hard to hang on to his belief in himself as a valuable human being. He was further hindered at home by parents who had difficulty in seeing his value. Nor when living at home could he reassure himself that he was liked by a group of friends. Even today, at nineteen, much of his work at college still focuses on his areas of difficulty in the basic three Rs. The saving grace for Tom was probably his popularity with most teachers. His most recent one made it very clear to him that she didn't want him to leave and would miss him greatly.

Tom has particularly wanted me to mention in this book how much he loved and, since her death, now misses his Granny Rose (Nick's mother). This may well relate to the very unconditional love she was always able to give him. He remembers her as kind but strict, with a good singing voice and funny as well. She had a love that accepted him as he was — a love that must have helped him through the hard times to believe in himself.

As I have become more aware of the importance of self-esteem, I have tried not to damage my children's view of themselves. I feel uncomfortable when I think of the hours I have spent telling Tom that his face needed washing, that his room was a mess, or that his clothes were inappropriate or dirty. When I shouted at him or ran him down , I could see him deflate and feel less adequate. I can now see how empowering it is to him when I comment on the positive things he does and how he then can respond by taking charge of other areas. I wish I had started off as a mother with the knowledge I now have but I also know that it is not too late and that changes in my behaviour with the children today still pay dividends.

Self-esteem is also relevant when looking at parents and carers of the disabled. I have a friend whose son has dyspraxia (a problem which relates to perception and movement). Like Tom, this condition took many years to diagnose. During that time she remembers the frequent reassurance from doctors and teachers, 'Don't worry so. He's fine.

He'll be all right.' She describes hearing this time after time after time, with the unspoken message carried with it: 'Stop being a fussing and neurotic mother.' If the mothers of the disabled do not fuss and push for understanding, nobody else will, but how damaging it must have been for her self-esteem. She also remembers a headmistress saying, 'The trouble with you is you always look so worried,' the impli-cation being that she was the problem. Time, and many reports and tests, proved that she had been right to worry. Now she regrets that when people said these things to her she was not as assertive as she now is. She would have replied, 'Of course I'm worried. Sit down and listen to me. I am with my son all the time and I'm worried about this, this and this.'

In my situation, it wasn't easy to like myself when I thought I was failing to love my son in the way I felt I should. I believed that it is a mother's role, if not her duty, to love her children. I found unconditional love very elusive and this undermined my feeling of self-worth. Without self-esteem, it is very hard for the parents and carers to speak up clearly for what they think is right or needed for their child. Nor is it easy for them to foster and protect their child's self-esteem.

We were not helped in this area by criticism from some teachers. One friend told me that she had met Tom's head-mistress at a party when he was about six. 'Tommy's great-est handicap is his parents. They are so understanding that he doesn't have to conform to the behaviour standards expected.' Time eventually proved that Tom had fundamen-tal difficulties that she was failing to diagnose but it didn't help our self-esteem to know that these things were being said about us. It amazes me how often, in parents' stories, this scenario seems to be repeated. The friend with a child who has Prader-Willi syndrome, which was not diagnosed by her doctor until her daughter was eleven, describes being told by a previous GP that her toddler's problems were hers, the mother's, and to go home and pull herself together. How wrong he was and what harm a remark like this can do.

Beatrice, when asked to comment on her experiences, wrote, 'One of my relatives recently gave me her opinion of Tom's problems, saying that what Tom had needed as a child was more smacks and more hugs. I felt so frustrated with her because it made me think about the efforts my parents went to in order to help my brother. They were strict at home but on occasions where we would meet other people my parents obviously didn't want to create a great scene by forcing Tom to do something he didn't want to do. Many friends have commented that I have this amazing ability to switch off so that I can't hear anything except the person to whom I am talking. I'm sure that this concentration comes from sitting at meals when younger with Tom shouting and demanding our attention, while the three of us attempted to continue our conversation. In public we would try and avoid such scenes, but as a result I am sure my parents were viewed as too lenient.'

Luckily, today I feel good enough about myself and my relationship with Tom and how we handled a difficult time with little outside assistance and I can hear remarks about Tom needing more smacks without immediately feeling a failure. I can acknowledge that we might have done better but that at the time we were doing the best we could.

When looking at self-esteem it is important to return to the three models of viewing disability — medical, charitable and social — and see the variable amounts of harm the different definitions have the potential to do. The first two (medical and charitable) disempower the disabled and damage their belief in themselves because outside able-bodied people are needed to 'save' or 'cure' the person. Under these definitions, disabled people are unable to rescue themselves without either a medical training or a large private income. The third model, which values all that they have to offer society, empowers them and begins the process of rebuilding their self-esteem.

I have found it intriguing to discover that, while writing

this book, I have a couple of times commented on my lack of contact with disabled people in my childhood. In fact it suddenly dawned on me that disability was a constant factor in my life as my father was blinded during the Second World War, a few years before my birth. Somehow I didn't see him as disabled, although I'm quite sure that my mother was very aware of it, given the changes she experienced. I think that the reasons for my attitude towards him were twofold. First, he was my father and I had never known any other type of father, so I accepted him the way he was. Second, I was instinctively viewing him from the perspective of the third definition of disability, the social definition. He had lost his eyeballs as a result of a bullet wound so the doctors were never in a position to 'cure' him. Nor did he need charity. He had qualified as a solicitor before the war, and although the support of the St Dunstan's charity for war-blinded servicemen was welcome, we were never dependent on it. My father, with a secretary who read his documents to him and a companion or driver to help him get to work, was able to earn a good living. He was, therefore, valued as a contributing member of society.

By working with the concepts of affirmations and self-esteem, my belief in the power of words has grown and, as I have written this story, I have become less and less comfortable using the word 'disabled'. I know that words move and change. (It is one of the beauties of the English language, that it is so flexible.) Words that seem neutral, when first used, become linked to prejudices and attitudes. Even though I have often found it hard to start with, I have supported the changes such as from mongol to Down's syndrome and spastic to cerebral palsy, especially when I hear my daughter's friends insulting each other's clumsiness by calling themselves 'spastic'. I expect these words will be changed again as society's attitudes move. I have also met the absurd side of political correctness around the use of words. In the Probation Service, I was once told off for offering to make a black student a cup of black coffee and I have

had a good laugh when Nick is referred to as 'follically challenged'!

The problem, for me, with the word 'disabled' is that it
does not start as a neutral word but instead defines the person by the things that they cannot do, thus disempowering
them at the same time. No wonder we and other parents
have found it hard to accept the idea of our child being disabled. Tom has never liked the word either. It was much easier to use the phrase 'special needs' even if it was such a wide
and bland term that it masked the reality of his problems.
American friends recently told me that in the States the
expression often now used is 'differently abled'. How well
that describes Tom. It immediately emphasises the areas in
which his strengths lie. His ability, for example, to break
through social inhibitors and meet people with a real link-
ing of hearts. I also think of his knowledge and enthusiasm
for Indian musical instruments. A combination of these two
strengths have resulted in his friendship with a Sikh family
near London. Nick and Tom visited their musical instrument
shop in Southall one day and, because of his pleasure in what
they were selling and his openness to them as fellow human
beings, they have become good friends of his and often invite
him to spend the day with them in their shop.

It seems that there are still moments when we can resort
to the old, discarded words. We benefited from the use of
the phrase 'mentally retarded' on one occasion, long after it
had been, quite rightly, discarded. It helped us to release our
unrealistic expectations of Tom at the time but, like the word
disabled, it is a negative definition and I much prefer 'differently abled' with the power that it offers the individual.

Twelve

Different paths

Living with Tom has created ample opportunity for all of us as a family to learn and grow and I have already mentioned some of the lessons we have gained. I grew up in a home setting where there was a considerable amount of shouting and quick temper. We expressed our anger at full volume after which most of us immediately forgot it. I thought this was the normal way to behave until I married Nick. If I shouted at him too loudly, he sulked for three days. I hated this, so had to start to change. Next, Tom came along and I really had to learn self-control. Even today, if I show any irritation with other people while out with Tom, he promptly verbalises my feelings with a few hand gestures thrown in for good measure. When driving, if I comment crossly on another road user, the next thing I know is that Tom will be waving his fist or doing a V sign — not advisable in this era of road rage! The end result is that I am far more patient than I was and my ability to stay calm in times of stress has improved.

Growing up alongside Tom has given Beatrice ample opportunity to watch and study his approach to life. She writes: 'I think Tom has the ability to bring out the best and worst in me. When I was younger, part of me felt this great desire to help Tom and I would try to give him reading lessons or teach him other things, although my patience was not brilliant. But there was another side of me which was quite antagonistic towards Tom and I knew exactly how to get a rise out of him. He had little control of his emotions and would react immediately and probably then be told off by our parents.

'Learning to gain a certain degree of self-control has been a difficult task for Tom but my friends, who only see him occasionally, are always amazed by the progress he has made. Tom found violence on TV impossible to handle, reflecting the fact that in life he would always be triggered off by strong emotions. I remember one evening Tom was watching *One Flew Over the Cuckoo's Nest,* which is a very disturbing film and totally unsuitable for him to watch. When he started to shout and leap about, my father tried to switch off the film and Tom began yelling and ended up stabbing the video machine. Such behaviour is unacceptable, but knowing how to deal with it isn't easy either.

'As Tom's emotions are so transparent, I find I learn a lot about feelings in general, which we so often go to great pains to conceal. Obviously we do need to filter and control much of what we are experiencing internally, but so often we don't even acknowledge that we have these feelings. Tom, on the other hand, deals with them instantly and then moves on. He also functions like an emotional barometer and will pick up on the atmosphere amongst those whom he is with and act accordingly. If we are tense, then Tom will be much more difficult and thus he can help us to gauge our emotions. It is a fine line between learning self-control and expressing one's feelings. I often catch myself bottling up emotions or not saying what I really feel because I'm afraid of the consequences and I think a little of Tom's candour would come in very handy!'

Beatrice is right. Tom is so open with his feelings. If he likes someone, he tells them so and frequently surprises people with a hug. I can feel myself blossom each time he unexpectedly says, 'Mum, I love you.'

I have described how we learnt to release our expectations around Tom and how his future would turn out. This lesson has spread to other areas of my life and I am better at 'going with the flow' rather than planning every detail. It is a much easier route through life and I am thankful that I had to change. I have also, to some extent, been able to release my expectations of myself as a mother. I have recognised that I have my limitations, shown to me by my feelings of helplessness, anger and frustration, and it is liberating to know where these limits are. I have let go of the idealisation of motherhood which at first undermined my role with Beatrice. I didn't achieve a natural childbirth or breast-feeding and saw myself as a failure. I now know that I cannot make everything right for Tom, cannot protect him from all pain or lead his life for him. However I do recognise that this doesn't stop me from being a 'good mother' and I am able to value the job I do.

One friend described herself as an able child coming from a very able family, brought up with an elitist attitude to society. Living with her disabled son, she has learnt to value all people, whatever their apparent limitations. 'My son,' she told me, 'opened my eyes to a whole world of difference. I remember being very unkind to a slow girl in my childhood. I wrote her off. Having Daniel for a son completely, radically extended my appreciation that everyone is unique. You don't have to get to the top of a mountain to succeed. Daniel is taking a different path through life. He has challenged my own judgemental self very deeply, the part of my thinking which writes people off.'

I can identify closely with this change in her, having been brought up to measure people by their examination grades, job status or even the cups they have won in sports. I, too, can remember a girl from my childhood whom I belittled and ignored because she couldn't run as fast as I could. Gentleness, humour, openness and sensitivity are now of far greater importance to me.

Beatrice gave me some further food for thought around this subject when she wrote a description of a recent visit Tom made to her in Oxford. 'It went extremely well and all my friends took a real shine to him, with the Dr Who catchphrase "You dare defy the Dominator!" remaining imprinted on their minds. On one of the days, Tom and I had lunch in a college where a physicists' conference was taking place. The lady in the canteen took one look at Tom's tweeds and bow tie and asked me if he was another of them. I looked round the room and realised that it was full of similarly attired tweedy types. Tom picked up on this and said how much he'd like to have been one of them.'

Seeing his older sister's achievements, with her long trips abroad and university life, has at times been difficult for them both, as Tom is well aware of his own situation. Despite being surrounded by ostensibly high-achieving people, Beatrice has found a useful reminder that exam results are not really so important. She writes: 'When I was anxiously awaiting my degree results a few weeks ago, I went to collect my brother from school in Brighton and attended his leaving ceremony. All the children without exception received certificates of achievement, a few for public exams but mostly for things like going on an activity holiday in France. I realised that my results were no different from those children's awards, which were a reflection of the time and effort they had put in. How relative all this success business really is. What I also see is that Tom is a wonderful, lovable person and that I do not need to judge other people or, as is mostly the case, myself on outward achievement, which is usually very transitory and flimsy anyway.'

A major lesson I have learnt from Tom is to value the unconventional. From my rigid start, dismissing the unusual, I have moved so far. When he started at boarding school and was described with obvious delight as an eccentric, I began to value this aspect of him. Our holiday in Egypt was considerably enhanced by Tom's ability to cut away the facade of expected behaviour. Through Tom I met and talked to people who would have remained strangers to me if I had been on my own. I still have a little way to go in appreciating his unconventional (or maybe over-conventional) style of clothes, but I doubt if I am the only mother to say that. In Tom's case it is not a punk hair-do or rings in his nose. He is a leftover from the 1930s with his waistcoats, stiff collars, ties and plus fours!

Though making some strides in this area, I still see myself as fairly conventional, which made me laugh when I read some more about the lessons that Beatrice feels she has learnt through living with Tom. She writes: 'As I grew up and became more self-conscious, I remember becoming acutely aware of Tom's behaviour in public and often being terribly embarrassed. Even now I can see that living with Tom is teaching me to release my narrow ideas of 'fitting in'. At the stage when the great concern of most young teenagers is to be the same as everyone else, especially when I moved to a conservative girls' school, I found my unconventional upbringing and 'wacky' parents quite a challenge. And Tom proved to be another. I remember, so vividly, crumpling with shame when Tom ingenuously asked our elderly Sunday School teacher if the hair around his penis was as white as the hair on his head.'

She continues: 'Now I find it easier to appreciate the freshness of MOST of Tom's slightly more controlled comments. I still struggle somewhat in other aspects of my character such as patience and acceptance, which I can see so clearly tested in my relationship with Tom. I remember finding him quite overwhelming. In fact I still do at times, as he has such a gargantuan presence which you have to experience to really appreciate. I still find my ability to listen to him talking repeatedly about the Daleks or Patrick Troughton is limited. On the other hand, Tom's incredible store of curious information often astounds me, along with his razor-sharp long-term memory.'

Thirteen

The top of the mountain

Much of this book is about 'reframing'. It's a word I am really enjoying at present. If you put a picture into a new frame, it can look totally different, even transformed. From one direction a situation can look like a tragedy. Viewed from another perspective, it is nothing of the sort. Reframing, as I use the term, is the art of changing the angle from which we assess things. I haven't read the textbooks that I know exist on this subject but I find it a powerful and inspiring concept. It is useful both for big issues and for small ones.

When I was deciding recently to leave the Probation Service, it was not an easy process. I was held back by the thought of the expertise I would be leaving behind. Then I changed my viewpoint and wrote a list of the skills I would take with me. Instead of seeing my career as a probation officer as a closed and discarded chapter, I saw it as part of the groundwork for the next stage of my life. I was then able to look forward and plan how I would use the future.

Mental disability can be viewed as a tragedy — or not. As long as it is regarded as a tragedy there is little escape. Certainly that was how we saw it when we at last accepted the doctor's diagnosis when Tom was twelve. It was also, probably, one of the reasons we took so long to recognise the full situation. The different definitions of disability I have written about are alternative ways of framing the concept. By reframing our experience, we have transformed it. We can now see a much more complete picture of Tom which includes all his strong points and gifts. We have, in fact, not just reframed the big picture of him, but also many of the experiences we went through with him. For example, we no longer see the searching we did for the right school as a waste of time, but as an opportunity to widen our knowledge of available types of facility and a chance to meet interesting and enjoyable people.

While lack of an understanding of number holds major problems for Tom, especially in relation to time and money, and he will probably need a trusted friend or relative to help him financially all his life, it also frees him up from so many of the heartaches and burdens that most of us have to carry around. Imagine life without money worries, with a belief that it is always available from a hole-in-the-wall cash dispenser! Imagine it without the pressure of time hanging over you. There are definitely plus sides to the way Tom experiences life.

When Nick looked back over the years with Tom, he described the stages we have gone through as shock, depression, frustration and embarrassment, followed by fascination and celebration. This doesn't mean that we never now feel the earlier emotions but that we have reached the point when we can, most often, celebrate Tom. We both feel that the largeness of Tom's personality and being is so much greater than his limitations. It makes us realise how we often define ourselves by our limitations — by what we cannot do. Tom's presence, the richness and fullness of his character, demonstrates that we can shine despite our limitations.

I am very aware that what I have written so far is only part of a story. No conclusions have yet been reached. We are currently in a new stage in Tom's life. He has finished with boarding school and in a few weeks will start his next course on 'Skills for Living' at our local college and so be at home with us. We will all need to readjust to this changed situation.

Last week he set off for his month in Kenya, wearing his beige summer suit, tie and panama hat with a feather in the band. He felt he really looked the part for his safari. He managed to reach the airport without panicking and, when the time came to say goodbye, kissed us and strode off with the airline escort, not even giving a backward glance. For Nick and me, it was a wrench to see him go. I have to admit I cried.

We haven't heard how the adventure has progressed as the phone system seems to play up. We are presuming that all is well. Now that I can see his strengths and the gifts he has to offer, I have confidence that his visit will be good both for him and for those he meets.

As I think over our life with Tom so far, the picture that comes to mind is of the party game 'Pass the Parcel'. Each time the music stops, the person holding the parcel can unwrap another layer. Each time you hope you have reached the gift. Throughout Tom's life, I kept thinking that I knew him but then the situation would alter. At different phases the paper changed. Tissue paper for the baby boy we were so thrilled to have. Dull brown paper as we realised that all was not well. Sometimes our gift seemed to be wrapped in nothing but newspaper as we struggled to value it. Nowadays, most of the time, the paper has become the expensive, strong, colourful kind that you buy to wrap a present for a special friend. I know there are still more layers to discover, but we have occasional glimpses into the gift at the centre, where a strong, spiritual being resides.

Tom enjoys a church service, especially as it is a chance to wear a suit and see his friend, the vicar. Beatrice meditates daily and attends Buddhist retreats and Nick finds his spirituality in his daily living. I have never fully recovered from the boredom of church services in childhood and prefer to meditate on my own when I feel the need. Recently I have found an inner guide from whom I gain great strength and wisdom. I'm not sure how I can define this Being — my Soul, my Higher Self, a wise part of me. If I were a born-again Christian, I would probably recognise it as the Christ. This entity, if I take the time to stop, ask and listen, can give me wise advice. The method that I find easiest at present for making contact is to sit still and relaxed, with eyes closed, and to visualise myself climbing a mountain. At the top I always find this friend.

Filled with enthusiasm for this type of meditation, a few months ago I encouraged Nick, Fiona and Tom to join me one evening to try this way of contacting our guides. It was the experience that followed, and the words that Tom had to say, that inspired me to write this story and through writing it to 'reframe' and 're-evaluate' our lives together.

We decided beforehand to climb our individual mountains and ask whoever we met at the top what was the purpose of our lives. Afterwards we shared our thoughts with each other. Tom had climbed a Scottish mountain and met his wise being in the guise of William Hartnell, the first actor to play Dr Who! He told us clearly and with a language unusual for him that the answer to his question was: 'I am here to show the world that I am lovable the way I am.' Suddenly my eyes were opened and I understood the main lesson he had been offering me all along — to love and accept him as he is and not to expect him to change to suit my needs. It is so simple and obvious to me now, but I needed him to spell it out to me before I could see it for myself. I know others who have learnt the same from him. He has been, and continues to be, a very good teacher for us all.

Afterword

Tom returned from Kenya delighted with his trip and with himself. No major mishaps occurred, despite a twelve-hour unscheduled stop in Mombasa due to an air traffic control dispute.

The two host families kept a detailed diary of each day's events, which helped to satisfy our need as parents to know how Tom spent his time and acted as a useful prompt to glean further information from him. Letters from his hostesses, sent on his return, indicate the success of the trip. Beldina wrote, 'We were very, very happy when Tom was staying with us. Tom is a good boy, friendly and very intelligent. Tom left behind so many friends who are still asking me when he will come back. He left a very big gap in our house. He used to call me Mother Beldina and my children his brothers and sisters. In fact we love Tom.'

Jane's letter said very similar things, as Tom had obviously won his way into the hearts of her family as well. 'We have been very happy and Tommy is a very happy boy. I think he has enjoyed the visit and he promised to come back again. We enjoyed staying with Tommy together and we did not want days to go. It was very sad for the whole family that Tommy has to leave but we pray God until we meet again.'

The success of the trip has definitely increased his self-esteem and confidence, which is already showing in small, but significant, ways. He has recently started his new course and his growth in confidence is, perhaps, reflected in the fact that he no longer needs to wear a jacket and tie on all occasions and sets off to college in much more casual and, to my mind, more appropriate clothes. He has also shown signs of wanting to take more responsibility for his life by setting his own alarm clock, shifting himself out of bed, sorting his clothes and PE kit and generally being ready for his taxi in the morning. It is, in fact, a big change rather than a small one.

We all, as a family, still have adjustments to make to increase our enjoyment in living together — but I really feel now that we are on the right path and are getting there fast.

Beyond this book, Henrietta Rose wishes to extend support to parents in a similar situation. To this effect, Findhorn Press and Henrietta have set up a special web site:

http://www.tom-giftindisguise.com

as well as a cyberspace mutual support group via email. Please visit this web site and join the chat group if you can either benefit and/or contribute to it.

If you do not have access to the web but are on email and wish to join the support group, please send a message to Henrietta on:

join@roses.prestel.co.uk